The Prisoner Of Zenda

Adapted by
Matthew Francis

from the novel by
Anthony Hope

Samuel French - London
New York - Toronto - Hollywood

THE PRISONER OF ZENDA

This adaptation was first presented at the Greenwich Theatre, London, on 17th December, 1992, with the following cast:

Black Michael	Nicholas Gecks
Colonel Sapt	Michael Cronin
Prince Rudolph	David Haig
Fritz von Tarlenheim	Tom Bowles
Rudolph Rassendyll	David Haig
Harry Burlesdon	Duncan Berkshire/David Wilson
Robert, Earl of Burlesdon	Timothy Block
Rupert of Hentzau	Mark Lockyer
Child at Station	Duncan Berkshire/David Wilson
Father at Station	Alan Cheeseman
Antoinette de Mauban	Melanie Jessop
Princess Flavia	Leonie Mellinger
Johann	Timothy Block
Josef	Nicholas Hall
Marshal Strakencz	Alan Cheeseman
Edward VII, Prince of Wales	Timothy Block
Detchard	Nicholas Hall
Bersonin	Timothy Block
Station Master	Alan Cheeseman
"Double"	Alan Cheeseman
The Boar	Michael Budmani

Director	**Matthew Francis**
Designer	**Lez Brotherston**
Music	Mia Soteriou
Fights	Malcolm Ranson
Lighting	Mark Henderson
Sound	Steve Huttly
Choreography	Jeff Thacker
Assistant Designer	Gideon Davey
Fight Captain	Nicholas Hall
Production Assistant	Rachel Kavanaugh
Deputy Stage Manager	Leighton Vickers

SYNOPSIS OF SCENES

ACT I

ACT II

Time: the turn of the 20th century

PRODUCTION NOTES

It is essential that Prince Rudolph and Rudolph Rassendyll are played by the same actor. The tricks played on an audience as a result of this "double" are the source of one of the play's principal theatrical pleasures. The production will require a virtually non-speaking stand-in—who must be the same height and build as the actor playing Rudolph Rassendyll and Prince Rudolph. Before Rassendyll goes to Ruritania the actor playing Rassendyll/The Prince will have a series of quick changes involving costume and moustache. The actor's red hair (or wig) will be unruly or well combed if time allows. In Scene Six—and up to the point where Rassendyll and the Prince confront one another in Scene Seven—the audience should not realise that a stand-in is from time to time being substituted for the principal actor. Prince Rudolph's entrance on page 21 should really surprise an audience. I fear this means no credit for the stand-in on any cast list. After the audience appreciate that there *is* a stand-in, the rest of Scene Seven and all of Scene Nine are spent teasing the audience with on-stage switches between the two actors. The entry of the boar allows for the first of these to be unexpected. Thereafter an audience likes to see how often Rassendyll can change into the Prince (and vice versa). The song on page 27 provides several opportunities for this.

The playing style should be full-blooded but absolutely straight-faced. The adaptation will only work if the characters speak with complete, unflinching conviction. We enjoy old movies because the actors deliver their lines with passion and sincerity—no matter how strange these lines sound to us now. When Rassendyll replies to Antoinette's "Impossible" with "Not, I assure you, for an Englishman"—he means it from the roots of his being.

There should be a lot of music throughout the play—between scenes as well as underscoring significant moments. The music must be straight-faced too. There is a full score available for the play—which includes settings for the two songs. It is by Mia Soteriou and terms for its use may be obtained through Rachel Daniels at London Management, 2–4 Noel Street, London W1V 3RB (071-287 9000).

The two pieces of music used for the coronation sequence are both by Telemann. *La Réjouissance* (at the start of Scene 14) and *La Générosité* (at the end of Scene 14): both from his "Twelve Marches". Tapes suitable for use in the production are also available.

M.F.

This adaptation is dedicated to

PHILIP FRANKS and **JON PLOWMAN**

with grateful thanks
for all their help and suggestions

ACT I

Scene 1

The Royal Palace at Strelsau, Ruritania

A large, forbidding door leads to the King's private rooms. In the flickering torchlight, we can make out a portrait of the old King——its frame draped in black. Michael——the King's illegitimate son——is hammering on the door. He is cold, hard, impatient——crippled within and without. He wears glasses

Sinister underscore

Michael Rudolph! RUDOLPH! Let me see my father. The laws demand it. I shall be admitted. Rudolph!! Tell them to let me in. It is my *right*. Rudolph—can you hear me?! It's in the rules!!

The door creaks open. Colonel Sapt, a loyal servant of the old King hurries out—pale, angry

Sapt Your Royal Highness! Please. He's very near the end. Show some respect.
Michael What's that? Something to do with love? RESPECT!—WHY WON'T HE SEE ME? I'm his son as well. This is his last chance, Sapt . . .
Sapt He's with Prince Rudolph . . .
Michael *I know who's with him. All tears and snivel. The baby boy!*
Sapt (*shocked*) The Crown Prince!
Michael I'm *older*. I'm cleverer. I've got some good ideas. He's *nothing*—his father's last gasp . . .
Sapt You'll do yourself no good with this . . .
Michael That's nothing new.
Sapt He loves you in his way.
Michael NO. Not true! Not the way he loves the boy. *That's* his way of loving. Treats him like a little monkey. Up on his shoulder!
Sapt Rudolph will be the King.

Michael I'm just his *bastard*.

Sapt Your Royal Highness!

Michael A mistake. The good man's one permitted sin. AND LOOK! God judged it. Punished him with *me*.

Sapt (*simmering*) I'll have the King's guard see you to your rooms.

Michael Sapt, Sapt—LISTEN. The country's not united yet. Little tribes, little ambitions. You know it. You've read Hegel. The state: Man's highest aspiration. We could achieve so much, Sapt.

Sapt We can. We do.

Michael We're going soft! Order through strength. I've written about it.

Sapt (*coolly*) Yes. I'd heard.

Michael Organise. Line things up. *We're all too nice*. I have a detailed plan you see. Two volumes . . .

Sapt Don't tell me. I don't want to know!

Michael You're stuck, man. STUCK . . .

Sapt We live from day to day, your Royal Highness . . .

A sudden cry from inside. A murmur of voices. Far away, somebody calls out "Rex Mortuus Est, Rex vivat"

Michael Gone. Too late. He's gone. Ah no. NO! (*Grief and anger run through him. A spasm. He turns to the picture on the wall*) DON'T STARE AT ME LIKE THAT. You never looked at me before. I owe you NOTHING. YOU'RE DEAD NOW! LET'S GET RID OF YOU COMPLETELY!! (*He lays into the portrait with his knife—shredding it*)

Sapt (*hurling himself at Michael*) Stop it, damn you. STOP IT!

Michael (*pulling away, suddenly quiet. Muttering*) Where's my watch? What time is it? Two? Three?—back to work. I shall send for Antoinette, for Rupert. This is all very easy really. Plenty of night left . . .

The door begins to open again

Rudolph (*off*) Will somebody get me a drink?

The door opens wide. Rudolph, Crown Prince of Ruritania, walks through. He is restless, disconsolate, peevish and—importantly—clean-shaven

Another Courtier hovers in the shadows. It is Fritz Von Tarlenheim, decent, honest, a friend of Sapt

Michael my dear, what a row. You sounded like a revolution. Such a noise. Get me a drink one of you. Anything. Wine would be nice.

Michael (*under his breath*) Damn you.

Rudolph I suppose I can get at the cellars now. Somebody give me the key. So. Poor old Dad.

Michael TELL ME.

Rudolph Oh. Dead. Yes . . . yes—quite dead. In there. I think he'd be happy to see you now.

Michael I couldn't hate you more than I do . . .

Rudolph Bang, bang, bang. Wouldn't let him alone would you? Bang, bang, bang. LET ME IN. He deserved peace you know. After all that life.

Michael He might have had something to say to me.

Rudolph I don't think so.

Michael His blessing.

Rudolph Oh no. He wouldn't have done that. Would he? Really?

Michael I've stood outside for a lifetime. Watching you through a crack in the door. I've watched you sitting on your cushion— Warming yourself. LITTLE KING. Scampering around his ankles. Pampered, patted. How I hate you.

Rudolph (*after a moment*) He gave me this ring. And he kissed me. And I told him how much I loved him. And he told me that it was all mine now. The bricks and the soldiers and the good old dogs. And you.

Sapt (*warningly*) Your Majesty . . .

Rudolph I like the dogs best. Strelsau wolfhounds. Fine muzzle, strong, fast. Coats like silk. Good dogs to be seen with.

Sapt You should sleep now. There'll be work in the morning.

Rudolph My dear Sapt, I'm not in the least tired.

The sound of religious singing. Plain-chant

. . . ah, the priests. Got their hands on him. (*A beat*) Couldn't somebody get me a glass of wine? I've asked you twice already. I'm not a child anymore.

Sapt (*without moving*) Sire.

Rudolph (*shouting*) Get me something to drink!! NOW!! For the King . . . The King wants a drink!!

Michael Not yet.

Rudolph My brother speaks. Would you make a note of that Sapt? He says—NOT YET.

Michael You're not King yet. Not until you're crowned . . .

Rudolph Yes, yes.

Michael . . . Not for another month. After due mourning. After the burial. Or would you rather not bother with all that. Such a bore. Why not open a few bottles, get happy, TIP HIM IN THE LAKE!

Rudolph (*stung*) I loved him. He was everything. I still breathe his air. He made me look like him. Walk at his side. Hold his hand. He couldn't bear you! He couldn't bear your sour face. HE COULDN'T TOLERATE THE WAY YOU WALK. YOUR STUPID, UGLY LEG!

With a howl of fury, Michael is at his throat. Rudolph throws him off. A ragged exchange of blows. Sapt rushes forward. He and Fritz pull them apart

Sapt Your Majesty! Duke Michael!—scrapping like urchins by your father's death-bed . . . *Shame* on you!

Fritz Please. Please, your Majesty . . .

Sapt (*to Fritz*) See Duke Michael to his rooms. I'll stay here with the Prince.

Fritz steps forward to help Michael to his feet

Michael (*sharply*) No! Don't touch me. I can manage. You see? I'm perfectly all right. Just out of breath. For a moment.

Fritz I'll come with you.

Michael Not a bit of it. Stay with his Majesty. Get him his drink . . .

Rudolph (*breathlessly*) Now the dog has bit his master . . .

Michael Good night. Your Majesty. Colonel Sapt—forgive me. Tomorrow I leave for Zenda.

Rudolph Shall you be taking little Rupert?

Michael The Count of Hentzau is a friend.

Rudolph Jolly good. And such a charming fellow. Very handsome. Good to be seen around with.

Sapt (*warningly*) Sire . . .

Rudolph Quite a contrast—

Sapt Stop this!

Rudolph Yes, yes all right. Go away, Michael. Bed-time. (*A beat*) I'll send for you in the morning. So don't set off *too* early. Will you?

Michael turns and goes. Fritz von Tarlenheim follows at a distance

I'll sit with him a little, Sapt. Just send up a bottle of wine—I'll sit

with him until I fall asleep. Haven't the others finished in there?
Get rid of them. All those doctors and Bishops. Old, old, old. Tell
them to get out. Tell them to go away . . .

Rudolph walks uncertainly back through the door

The plain-chant fades with him. Melancholy underscore

Sapt The days of greatness are gone. Would that I had gone with
them. God help us now. (*A beat*) A full moon. Treacherous. Cold.
(*He shivers*) Work to be done.

Sapt goes

The music rises as the Lights fade

SCENE 2

The terrace of Lord Burlesdon's town house, London

*By a simple device, the flickering darkness of Ruritania turns into a
bright spring morning in London, England. On the terrace are daffodils
and garden furniture*

*Somebody is practising a piano in the house. Rudolph Rassendyll is
teaching his twelve-year-old nephew to fence. Rassendyll is alert, cheerful,
dashing and—remarkably like the Ruritanian Crown Prince. The one
difference is a well-trimmed moustache on Rassendyll's upper lip. Both
Rassendyll and Harry—the boy—wear gloves, masks, chest pads*

*Rassendyll's brother—Robert, Earl of Burlesdon—sits in a deckchair
reading* The Times

Rassendyll Now then! On guard! (*Patiently*) Disengage. Beat. Attack
in the line of quarte.

Harry does so

Good! Now. Parry septime. You threaten in the line of quarte, I
parry, you deceive the parry, I counter.

Harry does so

Very good. Remember—straight at the heart. Once more—on guard!

They go through the routine again, but this time Harry scores a point

Now just a moment . . .

Harry takes the opportunity to score another

Harry AND AGAIN!!
Rassendyll Aaahh! (*Appealing to Robert*) This is palpably unfair. He's smaller than I am. I can't see where he is. It's like fighting with a wasp!
Robert Horrid child. Flog him.
Harry If I were you, I'd supinate my hand a little more on the parry . . .
Rassendyll (*surprised*) Thank you. I will . . .
Harry And tighten the wrist a little as it turns quarte . . .
Robert The only answer is a sound beating. You have my permission, brother. There are canes in the vegetable garden, slippers under my bed . . . there's a cricket bat somewhere . . .
Harry Father . . .
Robert I seem to remember a cat o' nine tails hanging on the nursery wall.
Harry You're being silly.
Robert I have no wish to be silly, Harry. It is an affliction that comes with age.
Rassendyll (*starting to work out a new sequence of moves*) Now, what shall we do next . . .?
Robert Even *The Times* is proving too difficult for me this morning. What does it all mean?

Rassendyll tries out the new moves, but Harry has other things in mind

Harry Uncle Rudolph . . .
Rassendyll Harry.
Robert (*scanning the paper*) Zulus, Suffragettes, a man crossing the channel in a balloon . . .
Harry (*to Rassendyll*) Are you what they mean by "dashing" . . .?
Rassendyll Certainly.
Harry Like one of those musketeers?
Rassendyll Very possibly.
Harry Do you ever DO anything?

Rassendyll How do you mean?
Harry Do you just "knock around"?
Rassendyll Why should I *do* anything?
Harry It's true, isn't it?
Rassendyll Our family doesn't need to *do* things . . .
Robert (*lost in his paper*) Nottinghamshire wiped out by Lancashire,
Kent eliminated by Sussex . . .
Rassendyll Come on, do you want to try this?

Harry puts down his foil

Harry Mother says that you just "knock around".
Rassendyll Your mother is a saint.
Harry She's *always* doing things.
Rassendyll Learning the piano . . .
Harry But you don't *do anything!*
Rassendyll Quite right.
Robert (*surprised, interested*) . . . and—oh my goodness—the funeral
in Strelsau of Alexander the Fourth—"thirty years King of
Ruritania" . . .
Rassendyll (*suddenly alert*) Really?
Robert (*reading*) . . . Architect of a modern nation. Statesman,
philanthropist, reformer. Clearly a good fellow. Distantly related,
Harry.
Harry Mother says—
Rassendyll That I should get a job.
Harry That it's to do with your hair.
Rassendyll Ah.
Harry Which is red.
Rassendyll *Dark* red.
Harry And your eyes—
Rassendyll Which are blue . . .
Robert And the Elphberg *nose*, one of which—according to *The
Times*—has just breathed its last in the state rooms at Strelsau.
Harry (*on to something at last*) What *is* an Elphberg nose, Father,
and why does it stop Uncle Rudolph doing things?
Rassendyll Could I look at that paper, Bob?
Harry (*sensing a cover-up*) Mother wouldn't tell me either.
Robert You wouldn't understand. Harry.
Harry It's to do with girls then.
Robert Well, in a way. But not recently.

Harry *Tell me.*

An embarrassed moment. Robert doesn't find such conversations easy. Rassendyll enjoys his discomfort

Rassendyll *(beaming)* Yes, Bob?

Robert *(painfully)* Well. Yes. Back in sixteen ninety-four, the Lady Elizabeth—one of your more exotic ancestors, Harry—met a red-haired, blue eyed Prince from Ruritania . . .

Harry *(helpfully)* Principal rivers the Zilina and the Cotack.

Rassendyll Good!

Robert *(still struggling)* Well . . . they took a shine to one another and had a bit of a fling.

Harry *(after a beat)* That's a dance isn't it?

Rassendyll Not exactly.

Harry What is it then?

Rassendyll *(amused)* Yes, tell us, Bob . . .

Robert They fell in love. Like your mother and I.

Harry Oh no.

Robert Indeed yes.

Rassendyll And almost exactly nine months after the Prince first met Elizabeth she gave birth to a little girl. Who bore a startling resemblance to the chap from Ruritania. Dark red hair, blue eyes and the Elphberg nose. You see?

Harry *(after a beat)* And this was because they took a shine to one another—and had a "fling"?

Robert Precisely.

Harry There's something you're not telling me.

Rassendyll Harry—the little girl's father was not Elizabeth's husband. It was the Ruritanian Prince . . .

Robert And ever since the Prince's indiscretion, members of our family have been known to look like him. Red hair, blue eyes . . .

Harry And the Elphberg nose.

Rassendyll Just like me.

Harry I don't believe a word of it.

Robert I said you were too young to understand, Harry.

Harry Father!

Rassendyll *(suddenly)* I'd like to go there.

Harry *(excited)* Yes!

Robert *(suddenly in charge)* Harry, it's time for your tea.

There is a moment's resistance

Harry!

Harry lingers a little in the doorway before going

Rassendyll I've never been.

Robert What's that you say?

Rassendyll I've never been there. Not actually to Ruritania itself. All round the outside. Never there.

Robert Well, we never have, you know that. Family tradition.

Rassendyll I'd like to go.

Far away—another sort of music begins. A gypsy note

Robert You're putting things off again. I know that tone of voice.

Rassendyll Looking at things again, Bob . . .

Robert I could get you a post somewhere. You know that.

Rassendyll Mr Under-Secretary.

Robert I like work.

Rassendyll I'll go to the coronation. Write about it. An article for the Pall Mall Gazette. A book maybe.

Robert You're incorrigible.

Rassendyll I've two thousand a year and a roving disposition.

From somewhere—inside the house perhaps—we hear Harry's voice calling "Rudolph, Rudolph" and then a woman's voice echoing that

Robert Some of us recognise the duties of our position—you only see the opportunities of yours . . .

Rassendyll I think that, for me, opportunities are duties.

Robert Well then, be careful. No more scrapes. Do you promise?

Rudolph's name is called again—but this time by a man. It is faint and far away——wrapped in a breath of wind

Rassendyll How can I? That's the whole point of it somehow. (*A moment*) I'll do my best.

The music suddenly becomes very insistent. The Lights change

SCENE 3

Zenda. Night

Rupert of Hentzau has persuaded Michael out on to the castle walls.
They stand on an exposed ledge: the ground—a hundred feet below.
Rupert is handsome, vain, self-absorbed. The only priority he com-
prehends is the gratification of his own—sometimes exotic—whims and
desires. This—married to a quick intelligence—makes him an effective,
dangerous operator. Now—he is in a mischievous frame of mind-
dancing to the music. He waves a brandy bottle. Michael clings on

Rupert RUDOLPH! Rudolph—by God's grace—King of Ruritania!
Rudolph the Fifth. Unlucky Rudolph. But KING Rudolph
nevertheless . . .
Michael Rupert! It's a long way up.
Rupert Wonderful view! We can see the bits YOU got. The Zenda
bequest! Pile of old stones, drawbridge, small herd of arthritic old
boar, (*shouting*) and a couple of mountains.

There is an echo

Michael I'm going to be sick . . .
Rupert And of course—Antoinette de Mauban. He has the undying
affection of a beautiful woman. Strange to tell . . .
Michael How far will you go?
Rupert To the devil's dinner-table, your Royal Highness, and check
your seat there.
Michael We're going to fall!
Rupert No no no. Fly perhaps. Out into the night. (*He takes a gulp at*
the bottle) The brandy is finished. *Finished.* Good bye, good bye
bottle! (*He flings the bottle out into the night*) Try to hit the King!
His name's Rudolph . . .

There is a distant crash

Missed. Damn.
Michael You drank it all.
Rupert And would drink another, your Royal Highness. (*Pointing*
out an even more precarious spot) Up there, perhaps . . .
Michael (*quickly*) No! No. Stop now. Let's go back in. We need to
talk.

Rupert When does the beautiful Antoinette arrive? I long to see her again.

Michael She's not *yours* . . .

Rupert There's a girl for you. Fine, dark, slim. Great brown eyes. Deep wells into which any man might fall.

Michael Don't say "fall"!

Rupert I would fall if she would let me . . .

Michael Rupert!

Rupert Even if she wouldn't . . .

Michael She's *mine.*

Rupert Incredible.

Michael Have a care, Hentzau. I could shake you off.

Rupert Not up here.

Michael I'm still the next King's brother. Heir to the throne. You're lucky to be near me. Slithering around on a bit of real power. You love it . . .

Rupert But do you love Antoinette?

Michael At certain times of day. (*A beat*) But Flavia's the key to it.

Rupert (*musing*) At certain times of day . . . and what do you get up to?

Michael (*ignoring him*) If Rudolph's crowned—he'll marry Flavia. She'll soon be littering the country with his children, and I'll be outside the door again. You see, Rupert, it's opened a little. I'm nearly through the door. I'm so close it hurts.

Rupert Drive your spurs in, go at a gallop where the crowd is thickest, let the bullets graze your ear, savour the stench of blood on your coat. The moment breaks before you. Clear and cold.

Michael You'll be beside me. I'll have you for ever then.

Rupert Give me your hand.

Michael Back from the edge.

Michael pulls Rupert to him and clings on

Rupert We'll stop your brother being crowned. We'll show him up. We'll show that he's unfit. Then you can marry Flavia. The one you really want.

Michael Sapt will stand against us, so will Tarlenheim, Strakencz. A dozen of the others.

Rupert No fun if they didn't. There's got to be somebody needs chopping up.

Michael You're not really as nice as you look, are you Rupert?

Rupert Hardly possible, your Royal Highness.

There is a Black-out

This is immediately followed by the deafening sound of a train rushing by, whistle shrieking

SCENE 4

A Light comes up on Rudolph Rassendyll—in full travelling kit. The noise of the train continues under his speech

Rassendyll (*to the audience*) Arrived safely at Calais, and took the ten-fifteen to Amiens. Thirty minutes to visit old Puivert and demand a bottle of his matchless eighty-nine. Then the one-thirty to Paris—changing only at Beauvais—where Tonerre hides the last of Napoleon's own Cognac. A night at the Continental. Chanced on Araminta Featherly, who—yet again—refused my invitation to the Café St Pierre. I dined alone on oysters and Chablis—lost in the contemplation of an old romance. (*Pulling himself together*) Last night to Dresden and the opera. A superb account of *Don Giovanni* . . .

We hear a few bars from Don Giovanni. Rassendyll joins in softly. The opera fades into the noise of a busy station concourse and the tune from Don Giovanni is perhaps picked up on a barrel organ

At Dresden, our train for Strelsau was unaccountably delayed, and—while waiting for its arrival—I experienced two unexpected and inexplicable encounters . . .

The Lights come up on a busy station platform

Small Child (*pointing at Rassendyll*) Daddy, Daddy! I've seen him on the stamps. The new stamps. Look, look!!
Father (*abstracted*) Read your Baedecker, there's a good boy.
Small Child No, but really—it's him. With a moustache. The very same . . .
Father (*mildly exasperated*) Don't point Willy, it draws attention to your finger nails.
Small Child (*to Rassendyll*) Excuse me . . .
Rassendyll (*genially*) Hallo, there.

Small Child You're on my stamps aren't you?
Rassendyll (*after a moment*) Is this a game?
Small Child Only you've got a moustache—like Uncle Franz.
Rassendyll (*baffled*) Is there a password?
Small Child New issue. Papa got them for me.
Rassendyll (*hopelessly lost*) Jolly good.
Father Stop irritating the gentleman, Willy!
Small Child Do you know any good jokes?
Father (*dragging the child away*) Let's *try* to find your mother . . .
Small Child Goodbye, Rudolph.

Father and Child exit

Rassendyll Goodbye. . . . (*Suddenly realising*) HOW . . .?

But the Child has gone. Rassendyll is amazed. How did he know my name? Am I asleep? What day is it?

In going, the Small Child has bumped into an elegant and beautiful woman—Antoinette de Mauban—knocking her valise and causing it to spill its contents all over the platform

Antoinette Fais Gaffe!!! Moutard stupide! Meine Geduld jetzt zu ende ist!!

Amongst the tumble of belongings are trinkets, papers and a small silver Derringer. Rassendyll rushes to help. He gathers up one or two things, including the gun. As the two straighten up, Antoinette screams

Vachement formidable!!
Rassendyll I beg your pardon?
Antoinette Impossible!
Rassendyll Not, I assure you, for an Englishman.
Antoinette You wouldn't . . . It couldn't be . . . you wouldn't have the courage—
Rassendyll Forgive me madame, but our island race can rival any nation when it comes to courage or tenacity, we . . .
Antoinette (*somewhat calmer*) Remarkable. You could be . . . But you're not, are you? Though as God's my witness, you *could* be . . .
Rassendyll Rudolph Rassendyll at your service.
Antoinette Thank you, thank you. I—forgive me. I mistook you for somebody else . . .
Rassendyll Your passport, Madame de Mauban.

Antoinette Ah—my secret is out.

Rassendyll Your identity is safe with me, Madame.

Antoinette You're welcome to my identity—I try not to publicise my marriage.

Rassendyll I see.

Antoinette In any case, he's dead.

Rassendyll I'm so sorry . . .

Antoinette I'm glad to hear somebody is.

Rassendyll May I . . .?

Antoinette No. Thank you. I'm travelling to Strelsau for the coronation. I am a guest of Duke Michael—the King's brother.

Rassendyll Then I'm sure you'll have no need of this. (*He returns the gun to her*)

Antoinette (*momentarily embarrassed*) On the contrary—it will prove essential. How kind of you to help me Mr . . . .

Rassendyll Rassendyll.

Antoinette Mr Rassendyll. Where are you travelling, Mr Rassendyll?

Rassendyll To Zenda—where I intend to explore the hills for a day. I'd like to see the Rattenspitze Falls, and get a glimpse of the old castle. Then the next day to Strelsau for the coronation. Then on. (*A beat*) In search of adventure.

Antoinette An English d'Artagnan.

Rassendyll (*frowning slightly*) No, not at all . . .

Antoinette Pray, Mr Rassendyll, do you know our new King?

Rassendyll I never saw him. I hope to do so on Wednesday.

Again we hear the distant sound of gypsy music—mysterious and disturbing

Antoinette You have an exciting week ahead. Perhaps a surprising one. Be careful, won't you. In the hills I mean. The countryside is so dangerous—and the wild boar have tusks like sabres.

Rassendyll I trust that you will also pass an agreeable week in Strelsau.

Antoinette There's little chance of that.

Rassendyll But . . .

Antoinette No "buts", Mr Rassendyll.

We hear the sound of the train's whistle

I think our train is at last ready. Adieu. Unhappily we shall not meet again.

Rassendyll Goodbye. (*Calling after her*) And good luck!

The music swells

The Lights fade

SCENE 5

Prince Rudolph's apartment in Strelsau

Curtained, rather squalid. Empty bottles on the floor. The Princess Flavia—pretty, with an honest, intelligent look—is in the middle of a difficult—and rare—interview with the Prince. He is evasive, restless, slightly drunk

Flavia The funeral was magnificent.

Rudolph Whose?

Flavia (*patiently*) Your father's.

Rudolph Is he dead? No! How frightful. You'd better tell somebody . . .

Flavia The Marshal looked splendid. Black velvet, black plumes, the red rose at his breast.

Rudolph He smells. I had to stand next to him for an hour.

Flavia You must be very upset.

Rudolph Would you like a game of cards?

Flavia I like the picture of your father in the long gallery . . . I saw you there last week . . .

Rudolph Picquet? Bezique? What about Écarté? That's not a hint by the way.

Flavia (*with emphasis*) I can't *not* mention it. This is the first time I've seen you since . . .

Rudolph What do you want?

Flavia To talk.

Rudolph We're always talking . . . I saw you only last . . . it must have been . . .

Flavia Four months ago.

Rudolph Well. Four. I've not done much since then.

Flavia You went with the King to Falkenberg.

Rudolph Good, good—you know all about it.

Flavia Tell me what it was like.

Rudolph You've been there. You know. Big house. Shutters. One or two fountains. What do you want. A guided tour?

Flavia I usually sleep in the old Queen Mother's bedroom.

Rudolph Really.

Flavia Your great grand-mother.

Rudolph Is she? IS SHE? I never made the connection.

Flavia Listen. We've grown up together. Played together as children. We've been on holiday to the same dreary places. We even share the same dreadful relatives. Your father hoped . . .

Rudolph You're very good at this aren't you? The talk. My father— the one that's dead—always told me that you were very intelligent.

Flavia I'm not, your Majesty.

Rudolph Would you like to sit down? Didn't I say?

Flavia No.

Rudolph So. You're very intelligent. What's that all about? Maths? Ancient History? Capital cities of the world?

Flavia Your father wanted us to marry.

Rudolph (*a spasm*) Don't go on about it. There's a good girl. Didn't you say he was dead? The old dad? Gone away . . . weeks ago. Not important now.

Flavia I'm sorry.

A moment passes

Rudolph Sit down. Please. Sit down.

Flavia I remember seeing you with him at the Christmas Feast. Twenty years ago—maybe more. He carried you on his back for half an hour while he gave the St Stephen money to the Palace servants. After they'd bowed and he'd said something nice about their children or how cold it was, you bent over his shoulder and shook each one by the hand and said "You look very well from up here."

Rudolph What is this?! You're making it all up. Really—I hardly remember anything about him. Can't I be left in peace?

Flavia Yes.

Rudolph Or do you want to act it out? The Christmas scene, all over again. A little performance—just the two of us. I'll call Sapt. He can play my father. Sapt! Sapt!

Flavia *Please* . . .

Rudolph (*deflating*) No. All right. We won't.

Flavia This is hard work isn't it?
Rudolph Well. There it is. (*A beat*) I'll tell you something. I'm not up to it. Really. Our secret, yes?
Flavia Of course, of course. I'll put it under my pillow.
Rudolph Exactly. Tell the dogs.
Flavia How are they?
Rudolph (*suddenly right with her*) Very well, very well. Thunder is quite recovered. And Lilly is having puppies.
Flavia Lilly? Good . . .
Rudolph We've moved her bed into my room. I wait up most nights—just in case. We're hoping for eight.
Flavia That'll be . . . splendid.
Rudolph You can have one. The little one.
Flavia (*faintly*) Thank you.
Rudolph God, I'd forgotten. I ought to go and have a look. She appreciates it. Really. What time is it? I feed her, you see.

An uneasy moment

Well. Good night. I go hunting tomorrow. Yes. Good night.

As he heads for the door, Sapt comes through it in answer to the Prince's summons

Sapt Your Majesty?
Rudolph (*pushing past him*) Good night!

Rudolph exits

Sapt looks at Flavia enquiringly

Flavia I tried.
Sapt Yes. Yes of course.
Flavia He talked to me about the dogs.
Sapt The dogs?
Flavia His only friends.
Sapt Did he say that?
Flavia He didn't need to.
Sapt Give him another month—please.
Flavia Another month. And then?
Sapt Nobody will blame you.
Flavia I shall blame myself.
Sapt (*protesting*) Your Highness . . .
Flavia Good night Colonel Sapt.

Sapt Good night, good night.

Flavia (*at the door*) I won't give up.

Sapt (*touched*) Thank you my dear. Thank you.

And the Lights fade in a swirl of sublime-mountain-scenery music——which leads us into. . . .

SCENE 6

The Mountains

Sounds of a waterfall. Birdsong. Heavily dappled sunlight. The beginning of the sequence in which Rassendyll and his identically dressed stand-in prepare for the "surprise" appearance of Prince Rudolph in Scene Seven. Please refer to the introductory note. The stand-in should make the first entrance here, across the back of the set. Rassendyll is dressed in walking gear: plus fours, tweed jacket, hat, small haversack. He carries a pair of binoculars. Johann the guide is pointing out landmarks directly upstage and away from the audience

The music continues as an underscore

Johann Yes, Mr Rassendyll. The Rattenspitze Falls are due north of here—some forty minutes walk. If you stand there on the ledge you can just make out the noise of the water . . .

And the stand-in disappears off in the direction indicated. After a moment . . .

Can you hear it?

Rassendyll (*from off stage; delighted*) YES! Yes, I can. It sounds like a brigade at full gallop!

And Rassendyll appears from exactly the place the stand-in went off. He is in great good humour. He inspects the view out over the heads of the audience

Why it's *magnificent!* Look at it! *Look at it.* (*Cupping his hands to his mouth*) HALLOOO!!

We hear the echo

Every bit as good as you said it would be. (*He is moved to quote*

Wordsworth) "And mountains over all, embracing all; And all the landscape endlessly enriched, With waters running, falling or asleep . . ." (*Pointing*) Is that the Castle there?

Johann The Castle at Zenda, sir. You can see the keep from here—still in good preservation. And very imposing so they say.

Rassendyll It looks like a picture. So still. Corot or somebody. Is it far?

Johann Ten miles or more.

Rassendyll The Duke of Strelsau's country residence.

Johann Black Michael, damn him.

Rassendyll Johann!

Johann Forgive me, sir. Black Michael is no friend to us.

Rassendyll Black Michael?

Johann The Duke, sir. Zenda may look pretty enough from up here, but it hides some dark secrets—truth to tell.

Rassendyll I won't believe it. You can't tell me that anything sinister would survive amidst so much *beauty*. Look at it! The up and down of it, the depth, the colours. Lovely, lovely.

Johann We could do with a few more roads, sir. Come winter we're as good as cut off.

Rassendyll Ah. I shall make a note. I'm writing an article you see. For a newspaper.

Johann Indeed.

Rassendyll These forests are splendid. Ancient of course.

Johann The old gods went hunting here.

Rassendyll (*in an ecstasy of enthusiasm*) Of course they did. Delightful. It's oak principally, with some chestnut. One or two beech trees . . . (*He wanders in and out of the trees as he talks*) Johann—I shall linger here and sketch. You may return to the village. I marked our way here. I shan't get lost.

Johann As you wish, Herr Rassendyll.

Rassendyll Tell the charming Frau . . . (*he can't get at the name*) . . . that whatever she intends to cook for our supper, it won't be enough.

Johann *Cook*, sir?

Rassendyll Some hunter's stew, I guess. Hare, venison, haunch of wild boar . . .

Johann I think you're confusing her with an honest woman, sir.

Rassendyll Look at it! The wondrous vale, the woods immense . . .

Johann Good day to you, Herr Rassendyll.

Johann exits

Rassendyll Good day indeed, good day. (*And he starts to whistle*)

Rassendyll moves in and out of the trees—looking for the right spot from which to sketch the view

  At some point during this, the stand-in takes over and continues the whistling

The tune must be absolutely uninterrupted. The stand-in settles on the dappled forest floor, and—as a chorus of rooks suggests the onset of evening—he turns his back on us and goes to sleep. The Lights indicate a passage of time. We must never lose sight of the sleeping figure

SCENE 7

Music. Time passes. It is now later that afternoon. We hear voices approaching. Sapt and Fritz enter in full hunting gear. Both carry rifles

Sapt How could you miss a thing that size? Dammit Fritz, he was as big as a bull. Did you see those tusks?! Well—we've lost him now: disappeared into thin air.

Fritz I fear I gave the game away—so to speak.

Sapt Bang bang—he goes. Bang bang. Just as the King was lining up his shot.

Fritz An accident, my dear Sapt. The tension was too great. My finger jerked the trigger.

Sapt Thank God we're all still alive . . . Hey now, what the deuce . . . Who's this?

They have seen Rassendyll. A moment of astonishment

Fritz Fantastic. Impossible. Is it? I thought we . . .? (*He stares at his gun in horror*) Oh my God . . .

Sapt No, no Fritz. It's not, but damn me it's close. The devil's in it. Shave him and he'd be the King.

Fritz Who is it?

Sapt He's sound asleep whoever he is . . .

Fritz (*softly*) I'll try for his papers . . .

Sapt Careful! You'd better give me your gun.

Fritz (*very carefully feeling in Rassendyll's pocket*) Here we are.

Sapt Good man.

Fritz (*reading*) Rudolph Rassendyll. British subject. (*The name rings a bell*) Rassendyll . . . Rassendyll . . .

He gets up and in stepping backwards treads on the stand-in's fingers. The stand-in is immediately awake. Yelp of pain. His back still to us

Sorry! Sorry! I am sorry!

Sapt Really! Fritz . . .

Fritz My dear fellow, forgive me—how can I ever . . . are you all right? So clumsy of me. It was the left boot—the left . . . right—as it were—on your fingers . . .

Sapt Mr Rassendyll?

Fritz Yes, yes, Mr Rassendyll. We were simply checking your papers . . .

Sapt Just tell him who we are, Fritz.

Fritz Who indeed—to intrude on your slumbers so terribly. This is Sapt—

Sapt COLONEL Sapt . . .

Fritz And I am Fritz Von Tarlenheim. We are both in the service of the King of Ruritania.

The stand-in gets up, bewildered

Suddenly a voice from behind them. It is Prince Rudolph. His basic costume is the same as Rassendyll and the stand-in. He wears a big coat over his shoulders and he carries a gun. He is of course clean shaven

The audience now see that a trick has been played on them. If the stand-in is a good match for the actor playing Rassendyll/Rudolph, then the blocking for the next seventeen speeches can be quite natural

Rudolph Where the devil did you get to Fritz? Sapt? I was left completely unattended. A sitting target for . . . (*He sees the stand-in*)

Stand-in }
Rudolph } (*together*) Damn me, who the devil's that?

A pause. The stand-in bows

Rudolph Fritz, Colonel—who is this gentleman?

Sapt His name is Rudolph Rassendyll. He's from England, sire.

Fritz (*suddenly*) Rassendyll, Rassendyll!! That was Pogo Burlesdon's other name. I was at Harrow with—must be your cousin.

Sapt Burlesdon? *Burlesdon*?! Thunder and lightning why didn't you
say so before. This explains a good deal. You remember sire—
Rudolph the Third and his jaunt to London—what—a century
ago . . .

Fritz Getting on for two . . .

Sapt Left a Ruritanian stain on the Burlesdon clan. Shows itself from
time to time. Here's the latest blemish on the family tree . . .

Rudolph That's quite enough, Sapt. (*To Rassendyll*) Well met cousin!
(*He laughs*) A thousand crowns for brother Michael's face when he
sees the pair of us . . .

Fritz *If* he sees . . .

Sapt Which he *won't*.

Rudolph You shall dine with us tonight.

Sapt protests

Cheer up, Sapt! You don't meet a new relation every day.

Fritz We dine sparingly tonight.

Sapt With an early start tomorrow.

Rudolph How can I forget. (*A beat*) Come Sapt,—let's go back. We
must try to enjoy ourselves this evening . . .

*Suddenly there is a thunderous noise close to them in the forest. From
a thicket there appears a mighty boar. Fangs, slobber, red eyes—the
full piggy look. It squeaks and roars, pawing the ground . . .*

Fritz THE TUSKER! God in heaven—it's huge!!

Sapt The devil! Fritz!! Your gun. Use it!! Now, now, before it
tramples us . . .

Rudolph Quickly, quickly man!!

*Fritz's gun goes off with a deafening roar and a flash. The boar leaps in
the air and falls to the ground with a squeak. During all this commotion,
Rudolph rushes to the stand-in and they swop hat, gun, moustache etc, so
that when the audience look back, a coat-wearing, gun-carrying stand-
in has his back to the audience, and Rassendyll is facing us*

Sapt (*delighted*) Well done lad, well done!

Fritz At least we'll have something for our dinner . . .

Rassendyll A fine shot! Congratulations!

Sapt Point blank range of course.

Rassendyll (*turning to Rudolph*) Forgive me, your Majesty. I'm still
amazed. A man doesn't expect to see double at this time of day!

There is laughter

I shall be honoured to dine with you tonight. Re-united with your British cousins on the eve of your coronation. What better omen for the future of your kingdom. For the future of Europe!
Sapt Well said, doppelganger. I like the hang of your jaw. Fritz—get someone to bring that pig down. It's not far to the lodge, Mr Rassendyll. You go ahead with his Majesty.

And the two redheads walk off together, arm in arm and talking . . .

Fritz (*referring to Rassendyll*) What ARE we going to do with him?
Sapt (*referring to the boar*) Well—if I had my way—I'd stuff him with chestnuts.

A moment of incomprehension as the Lights fade and Antoinette's music fades in

Scene 8

Antoinette's apartment at Zenda

Firelight. A piano playing out of sight. Antoinette sings softly to the music which continues as underscore through most of the scene. The song is adapted from Flos Lunae *by Ernest Dowson*

Rupert is listening, unnoticed by Antoinette

Antoinette (*singing*) I would not alter thy cold eyes
          Nor have thee smile, nor make thee weep
          Though all my life droops and dies
          Desiring thee, desiring sleep.

          I would not alter thy cold eyes
          With trouble of the human heart
          Within their glance my spirit lies
          A frozen thing, alone, apart.
Rupert Beautiful.
Antoinette I didn't hear you knock.
Rupert I wanted to surprise you.
Antoinette But I'm not. Surprised I mean. I don't believe I could be.
Rupert Well, I'm glad you're here. It's a cold place. Michael doesn't want to celebrate.

Antoinette What do you mean?
Rupert The great event tomorrow.
Antoinette That's hardly surprising.
Rupert Don't you mind?
Antoinette Not in the least.
Rupert But then—he sends you presents.
Antoinette There. You know.
Rupert Every other day. A tiny flask of opium.
Antoinette Just big enough.
Rupert But only just.
Antoinette In Paris I rely on an old man near the Val-de-Grace. He is expensive, but the quality is good. Dealers are often unreliable, you see.
Rupert But why? Where do you go? Tell me.
Antoinette You wouldn't understand.
Rupert I might.
Antoinette I cannot live without it. It kills the pain that quarrels with my heart. It wraps me in stillness and lifts me into the air. The world falls into place. I have a purpose.
Rupert You know I get it for him.
Antoinette Well thank you, Rupert.
Rupert I've been watching you.
Antoinette Yes.
Rupert Good, you noticed.
Antoinette I've seen you lurking.
Rupert Waiting for you. Dance with me.
Antoinette Of course. . . .

They dance

Rupert Your eyes are so dark. How thin you are. You hardly eat.
Antoinette I hardly need to.
Rupert Is it that you want to die? I could arrange it. We could die *together—yes*, that's quite a thought—to kill you as the blood drains from my wrists.
Antoinette I see you, Rupert Hentzau. Even greedy for death. Just to see what it's like on the way down.
Rupert Oh, yes. I'd like that.
Antoinette Poor little boy. Convinced the world is everything he sees.
Rupert I know it is.
Antoinette If it's still, move it; if it's strong, attack it; if it smiles, make love to it. The world's played a good trick on you. Don't you mind?

The music finishes. A moment of silence

Rupert Kiss me.

Antoinette No.

Rupert You'll be amazed.

Antoinette You're in high spirits.

Rupert I'm looking forward to tomorrow. The coronation. (*With a smile*) Significant events.

Underscore. Distant, ominous

Antoinette Michael won't enjoy it very much.

Rupert Well, he might.

Antoinette He hasn't said a word about it since I arrived.

Rupert Really. Today he sent a present to the King, wishing him good fortune.

Antoinette A present?

Rupert A present that will end their quarrel.

Antoinette So. You're up to something.

Rupert But tell me—honestly. Michael's a poor creature don't you think?

Antoinette No.

Rupert Hardly better than his brother. You must be disappointed by him.

Antoinette No. Not at all.

Rupert You know that you can trust me.

Antoinette (*laughing*) Tell me first—what present did he send the King?

Rupert (*after a moment*) Good night, Madame.

Rupert goes

Antoinette (*calling, urgently*) Rupert! Rupert!

The Lights fade

SCENE 9

The King's Hunting Lodge. After dinner

We see the back of a high, deep settle, a couple of chairs, assorted hunting trophies. The fire is upstage, facing us. Rudolph and Rassendyll can swop useful indicators while sitting on the settle. They always sit together on this—Rassendyll with Rudolph. When either one emerges, he has on a slightly different costume: Rudolph is in a dressing gown or smoking jacket; one has a moustache—the other is clean shaven; Rassendyll is neatly combed, Rudolph is tousled etc. Occasionally we see the red hair or arm or leg of the stand-in, or all of him if Rassendyll or Rudolph are in full flood down stage. Obviously—to change over, both must be hidden. There is a servant—Josef. Sapt and Fritz are there too. Everyone is rather drunk, except for Rudolph who is very drunk

Rassendyll (*standing*) There are fifty Burlesdons hanging in our hall. Great big paintings. Rubens, Van Dyke—all those chaps. Forty-five of them without a trace of red. Not in their hair, not in their cheeks, not in their lips. Bloodless bloody Burlesdons. But five of the fifty are drenched in scarlet—fire and wine staining their woolly locks. They let the cat out of the bag. God bless them—and God bless you your Majesty . . .

Rassendyll collapses on to the settle next to the stand-in. Loud cheers and oyezs from the others. Josef creeps round giving out full bottles to replace the empties. As soon as Rudolph is ready—which with practice can be almost immediately—he should appear from behind the settle and head for the table of drinks

Sapt During the events of eighteen seventy—when the Ruritanian army distinguished itself in the European slaughter, and a new order was revealed—despite our best efforts to frustrate it —I had the honour to serve in the Second Division of the Strelsau Hussars at the battle of . . .

Rudolph Another bottle Fritz . . .

During the following Josef exits

Fritz (*speaking across to the more or less invisible body of Rudolph*) Remember tomorrow! Your Majesty. It's quite late . . .

Sapt That was our watchword—muttered between sentries at night: REMEMBER TOMORROW . . .

Fritz (*persisting*) Remember the coronation . . .

Rudolph Remember Master Fritz that you start before I do. You must be more sparing by two hours than I.

Fritz Mr Rassendyll—the Colonel and I leave here at six. We ride to Zenda and return with the Guard of Honour to collect the King at eight, and then . . .

Rudolph We all ride together to damnation . . .

The stand-in, as Rassendyll, stands up, near the fire

Sapt Peasants and rogues! Guard of Honour be damned—Black
Michael's thugs and ruffians. You know—it's true, Rassendyll,I
was the youngest man ever to command the Strelsau Hussars . . .

Rudolph (*to the stand-in*) Come cousin, no need for you to get up
early. Have some more of this. (*A moment*) Sing to us, Fritzy.
Something sad.

*Rudolph and Rassendyll both collapse onto the settle. During Fritz's
song, Rassendyll/Rudolph can appear two or three times, first as one
character then the other. Rassendyll would be up-beat and might try to
join in with the song. Rudolph would be moody and drunk. Sapt might
join in with the odd line. The song is adapted from* Flammonde *by Edwin
Arlington Robinson*

Fritz (*singing*) There came Flammonde, and who he was
    He never told us, or what cause
    Had banished him from better days
    To play the Prince of Castaways—
    And yet he played surpassing well
    A part—for most—unplayable.

    So noble, proud and unafraid,
    We were not certain that he played—
    How much it was of him we saw
    We cannot ever know—
    Nor cannot say how much we learnt
    From one who never will return . . .

Rassendyll (*in view, leaning over the back of the settle*) This wine is
beyond all price and praise. Let us do it justice.

Fritz (*getting unsteadily to his feet*) The magnificent Princess
Flavia—whom we fervently hope will soon be dressed in glory by
your side, your Majesty,—is served by a lady—the Countess Helga
Von Strofzin—who has a hand and an eye and a leg and—dear
God—a breast—

Sapt What happened to the rest of her, Fritzy?

Fritz Her breast is a hidden treasure. A secret rapture. See it, and
die . . .

Rassendyll No, no. See it and understand the absolute dominion of
love. (*He collapses back on to the settle*)

Josef reappears with a very dusty, old bottle on a tray

Josef His Highness the Duke of Strelsau bade me set this wine before
the King, and pray the King to drink—if he is able—the oldest
vintage in the vaults of Zenda.

Underscore. Mysterious, full of foreboding

Rudolph (*rising slowly*) Give it to me Josef. Did he think I'd flinch
from this? Give it here. Listen to me all of you. My father was
magnificent. He knew everything . . . saw everywhere. He was so
impressive—it overwhelmed you. I'll show him. I'll show you all
that I could do as much as he could. Any day. (*A beat*) Thank you,
Michael. (*He drains the bottle, the wine spilling over his lips and face.
When he's finished, the bottle falls from his hand, and slowly he
crumples over onto the floor—on the downstage side of the settle*)

*The underscore swells up. Fritz and Sapt fall into a drunken sleep. The
Lights fade down on them and in a momentary black-out, the stand-in
takes Rudolph's place on the floor*

*Immediately the lights come up on Scene Ten—a night-time scene at
Zenda. Scene Ten is super-imposed on the tableau left at the end of
Scene Nine*

SCENE 10

Somewhere in the castle at Zenda

*Michael appears—pale, confused, without his glasses. He feels his way
uncertainly along the wall. His voice is hoarse, a whisper. He is
frightened*

*Antoinette comes from another direction. She has a lighted candle. The
three figures from the previous scene lie like ghosts around them*

Michael Antoinette. Antoinette—are you there?
Antoinette Yes. Michael. Here.
Michael Suddenly I couldn't see at all. I lost my way. It was dark . . .
Antoinette Tell me.
Michael I didn't know what time it was. I heard the bell at two
o'clock, then at quarter past the hour. I was working of course,

thinking. But then I heard it *again* . . . the quarter hour. You see? I couldn't think what time it was. The light had gone. Someone had taken the lamp. . . .

Antoinette It's nearly four.

Michael It can't be. . . .

Antoinette Yes.

Michael What happened to the bell in the courtyard? It didn't strike the half hour, the three quarter hour. It didn't strike the hour at three. It must be broken. . . .

Antoinette No, Michael. I heard it.

Michael What was I doing then? Why didn't I hear it? Somebody must have played a trick on me. Some sort of drug. I couldn't hear.

Antoinette Michael. . . .

Michael And then of course, when the effect wore off—I thought I couldn't see. The candles had been taken.

Antoinette Michael, you fell asleep. The lamp went out.

Michael I'll change the guard again. Move them out. I'll bring men in from the Hussars. No one expects that.

Antoinette *You were asleep.*

Michael My eyes were open.

Antoinette But you were still asleep.

Michael I couldn't see, I couldn't hear. There were people in the darkness. One of them tried to take the lamp. They wouldn't let me know what time it was.

Antoinette There's no-one here. Everyone's asleep. You're safe.

Michael Yes . . . yes . . .

The four o'clock bells sound

Antoinette There. Can you hear the bell. It's four.

Michael Good. Good. (*A beat*) Why do they do this to me?

Antoinette You know. To test us.

Michael Yes, that's it.

A beat

Antoinette I'll help you back. Let me take your arm.

Michael Yes.

Antoinette You have so much to do.

Michael Never enough time.

Antoinette I'll help you.

Michael There are secret plans.

Antoinette Of course. Rudolph will fail. You must be ready.
Michael We shall be ready. Rupert says it's best that you don't know
about the plans. You'll be impressed. Nobody's been forgotten.
Antoinette Good. Good.
Michael (*floundering*) Antoinette.
Antoinette Michael—give me your hand.

And they go

Light fade to Black-out

SCENE 11

The King's Hunting Lodge

*The sound of a cock crowing. Dawn chorus. Early morning light streams
in. The stand-in—dressed as Rudolph—lies where Rudolph collapsed at
the end of Scene Nine. Rassendyll is just visible—asleep on the sofa.
Fritz is bent over the Prince—watching him anxiously*

Sapt enters with a bucket of water

Sapt We'll see what this can do . . . (*He hurls the water over the
stand-in*)
Fritz Nothing. Not a twitch.
Sapt Damn it and damn him. It was the last bottle—mark my words.
Fritz What's to be done?!

A snore from Rassendyll

Sapt Wake him.
Fritz NO, no,—surely it would be better if he . . .
Sapt Never mind. I'll do it.

He throws the rest of the water over Rassendyll, who comes to with a start

There!
Rassendyll What the devil . . .
Fritz It's five o'clock.
Rassendyll For God's sake! *I'm soaked!*
Sapt Nothing else would rouse you.
Fritz Rassendyll—forgive us, but we have a very serious problem on
our hands.

Rassendyll What's wrong?
Fritz (*pointing at the Prince*) Look here.
Sapt We've tried everything.
Rassendyll What's the matter with him?
Fritz Feel his pulse.

A moment. Rassendyll does so

Rassendyll Slow.
Fritz Very slow.
Rassendyll But I kept pace with him last night.
Fritz Except for the last bottle.
Sapt Sent by Black Michael.
Rassendyll What are you suggesting?
Sapt I don't know.
Rassendyll We must get a doctor . . . (*Suddenly remembering*) . . .
Dear God—the coronation!
Sapt He'll not move for a day. I know the look of it.
Fritz We must DO something . . .
Sapt (*drily*) By all means . . .
Rassendyll If he's not crowned today . . .
Sapt He'll never be crowned.
Rassendyll Now that's absurd.
Sapt Strelsau Cathedral. Packed to the rafters. Half the army outside
with Black Michael at their head, sword drawn, very much in
charge . . . Excuse me, your Highness, the King's drunk.
Rassendyll *Ill.*
Sapt They know his "illnesses" too well. He's been "ill" before.
Rassendyll But this time . . .
Fritz He's been drugged.
Sapt Hard to tell the difference, harder to believe it.
Rassendyll Do you believe it?
Sapt (*a moment*) Yes.
Rassendyll Who did it?
Fritz Michael.
Sapt I'm sure of it. Michael has a following. Malcontents—the men
his father kept in check. Enough of them to say enough of this. (*He
kicks Rudolph's inert body*) Tch! The drunken dog. But he's an
Elphberg—and the son of his father. If Michael gets on the throne,
we're for the dark ages.

A long pause

(*To Rassendyll*) You must go.

Rassendyll Where?

Sapt To Strelsau, to the coronation.

Rassendyll What?

Sapt (*quietly*) You must play the King.

Rassendyll You're mad.

Sapt Fate sent you here.

Rassendyll (*stunned*) Good God.

Fritz Of *course*!

Rassendyll OF COURSE?

Sapt Are you afraid?

Rassendyll NO! No. But it's impossible. They'll know it's not the King.

Sapt It's a risk against a certainty.

Fritz The certainty that if Prince Rudolph isn't crowned today . . .

Sapt He won't be crowned tomorrow.

Fritz If you shave, I'll swear you'll not be known.

Rassendyll You've taken leave of your senses.

Sapt (*very serious*) Listen Rassendyll. If Rudolph isn't crowned this morning, Michael will sit tonight on the throne of Ruritania. He'll soon be rid of us—Fritz, myself, a dozen others who believed in what the old King stood for. Then a cold wind will start to blow. People will lock their doors at night, put bars at their windows . . . Friends will disappear and not be seen again. Believe me, Michael's a queer fish. He has the eyes of a tyrant. We're in your hands, boy.

A long moment

Rassendyll I'll do it.

Underscore. Stirring; promising adventure

Sapt Good lad.

Fritz Now there's a chance!

Sapt Thank you.

Fritz Our English d'Artagnan!

Rassendyll What was that?

Sapt We must be quick. Listen. This is the plan. After the coronation we return to the palace for the Ball. After a decent appearance there, I'll say you're tired and you need your bed. You and I slip out by a back entrance and ride here at a gallop. Fritz will guard your room at the palace and let nobody in.

Fritz I can see that bit will be important . . .

Sapt Our lives depend on it!

Rassendyll And then?

Sapt The King will be ready. Josef will have prepared him. When *we* get there, he rides back to Strelsau with me, and you ride as if the devil were behind you to the fontier.

Fritz King for a day. It's like a fairy-story.

Sapt (*grimly*) Make sure it has a happy ending.

Rassendyll Please!

Sapt (*calling*) Josef! Shaving tackle. Fritz, help me to carry his Majesty down to the cellar. We'll lock him in and Josef here can deal with snoopers . . .

Fritz It's a risk . . .

Sapt (*roaring*) Of course it's a risk—you fathead. Dear God, it's all a risk. If they suspect, or prove he's not the man we say he is—we'll meet our maker later on today, so shot and stabbed we'll looked like two old sieves! Now listen Rassendyll, you've got a lot to learn . . .

And the scene disappears in a whirl of music

SCENE 12

The principal balcony of the Royal Palace at Strelsau

Assorted members of the Royal family are there. In the centre, but isolated from the rest, are Michael and Flavia. They are both on edge—for very different reasons. We hear the noise of a crowd, a brass band playing in the distance

Michael Forgive me for standing so close. I know it causes you distress.

Flavia Why should it cause me distress? Look at the people in the streets. How close they stand to one another.

Michael You could hardly be farther away.

Flavia (*ignoring this*) There are so many of them.

Michael You know my feelings for you.

Flavia *Please*. Not now—I beg you.

Michael (*after a moment*) There are indeed.

Flavia What?

Michael A great many people in the streets.

Flavia I think that some of them are watching us.

Michael They're too far off . . .

Flavia For what?

Michael They can't see how you're trying not to touch me.

Flavia Michael!

Michael The beautiful eyes fixed a little too wide open, the soft lips pressed together so the mouth is stern. A tiny pulse I've never noticed in the fine skin of your throat.

Flavia I'd rather you didn't speak to me like that.

A moment. Then Michael startles Flavia. He speaks in a bullying, contemptuous tone

Michael Wave to the people Flavia. They want to see you happy to be seen with me.

Flavia I don't believe they care.

Michael Many of them had rather you and I . . .

Flavia NO. Many of them are glad I know my duty . . .

Michael (*quickly*) It is a *duty* then.

Flavia Listen. At twelve o'clock the Prince will pass through the city gates into the old town. You will hear how the men and women of Strelsau receive him.

Michael I shall listen carefully.

Flavia As the clock strikes—the cheers and shouts of a loyal city will tell you how they love him.

Michael Let us hope that he woke up in time.

Flavia Colonel Sapt . . .

Michael Yes?

Flavia Colonel Sapt is with him. He will supervise arrangements.

Michael But I'm not surprised you're sad.

Flavia I never said that I was sad . . .

Michael He's just a child. Still little Rudolph.

Flavia If that's the case—why are you so frightened of him?

Michael And you'll be married to him—married to a child. Of course you're sad.

Flavia Please. Stop it.

Michael I'd keep him on a lead.

Flavia You'd like that.

Michael Tied up. Out by the kennels. Well, *he'd* like that—wouldn't he?

Flavia Why do you want me to think poorly of you? Why do we have to speak like this? We could talk about something else you know . . .

Michael Just a few seconds to go. He'll soon be riding through the city gates. Under the midday bell.
Flavia I could have been your friend.

Michael winces. Silence. Then after a moment . . .

Michael A complex mechanism—the city clock. It's wonderfully well ordered. Have you ever looked at it? Great springs and cogs and wheels—patiently creeping up on you, clicking round, nudging the hour into place. And then . . .

The chimes prior to the hour begin to sound

Flavia You don't want a friend though. You want servants and soldiers. I think you only like the army.
Michael (*faintly*) Yes . . .
Flavia Neat shapes and simple sums.
Michael (*distantly*) The great bell.

And the first stroke of the hour rings out a mile away. Silence. A second stroke. Silence

Michael (*breathing fast*) YES.

The third stroke. Silence

Flavia (*nervously*) You know something . . .

The fourth stroke, then the fifth. Suddenly a great cheer bursts out at a distance, and is picked up by the crowds nearer to the palace

There! You see? They're pleased to see him.
Michael Impossible . . .
Flavia We must join the procession. Rudolph is coming.
Michael NO. No, he isn't. It's not possible.
Flavia What are you dreaming?
Michael (*faintly*) There's something wrong. Something's gone wrong.
Flavia Everything is quite in order, Michael. The train arrived on time. The King was on the train. Your own Hussars are with him—and the whole party has just trotted in through the city gates. It's all in perfect order, Michael. Just as you like it.

Fast fade on the balcony

We hear a great riot of bells and cheering. A glimpse of flags and pennons. Then . . .

SCENE 13

Outside the Cathedral

Suddenly, before the great door of the cathedral, we see Rassendyll—splendid in white uniform, boots, ceremonial sword and coronation robes. He is, of course, clean shaven. He stares a little too rigidly ahead. Sapt and Fritz—in full dress uniform—stand on either side of him. Soldiers at attention in the background. Marshal Strakencz comes forward and kneels to Rassendyll, who looks nervously at Sapt

Sapt (*sotto voce*) Marshal Strakencz.

Rassendyll extends his hand. Strakencz kisses it and stands

Rassendyll (*feebly*) So many people . . .
Strakencz (*mildly surprised*) Of course, Sire.
Rassendyll (*making an effort*) Why are they kept back to the other side of the square?
Strakencz (*amused*) They were your orders, Sire.

Sapt and Fritz wince. Rassendyll saves the day

Rassendyll (*a lucky improvisation*) I've changed my mind. They must be allowed forward—to the steps of the Cathedral. I will have my people see their King trusts them.
Sapt (*in the tone he'd use for Rassendyll*) Is this wise?! (*Realising and changing gear*) . . . your Majesty.
Rassendyll (*bravely sticking to his guns*) Am I Crown Prince in this land or not, Colonel? Tell them!
Sapt (*chuckling*) Good, good. So be it.

He signals. The crowd cheer. Rassendyll waves

Strakencz Let us proceed into the Cathedral, Sire.

They turn back through the great door. The Lights immediately change to . . .

SCENE 14

The interior of the Cathedral

*Smoke from incense, stained glass, candles. A procession. The Archbishop enters in gorgeous array, attended by altar boys and other acolytes. They take up their position by the altar. Then we see Flavia, Michael and Rupert take up positions on either side of the main group. Rassendyll enters with Sapt, Fritz and Strakencz. The coronation anthem thunders out (*La Réjouissance *from* Twelve Marches by Telemann: see introductory note). *Rassendyll takes in a thunder-struck Michael, then—for a longer moment—the beauty of Flavia*

He moves on to the Archbishop and kneels before him. Altar boys arrange the coronation robe. The Archbishop raises the crown and places it on Rassendyll's head. Rassendyll stands, turns and—prompted by Sapt—puts out a hand to Michael, who comes forward and kisses it—reluctantly. He retreats, and Flavia comes forward. She kisses his hand, he raises her, they embrace. Together, they turn and move away from the altar

The anthem finishes, the lights dim. The party have arrived at a side-chapel where they relax for a moment before moving on to greet the waiting crowds

Flavia You look wonderful.
Rassendyll (*tentatively*) I am—a new man.
Flavia There's a light in your eyes. I don't think I've ever seen it before.
Rassendyll Thank you.
Flavia You're even looking at me.
Rassendyll (*immediately abashed*) I'm sorry.
Flavia No—please don't be. I'm just surprised.
Rassendyll (*with absolute candour*) I am as well. I'd not expected . . .
Flavia What?
Rassendyll To be so very glad to see you.
Flavia Well—that's honest I suppose.
Rassendyll (*hastily, formally—so that the others can hear*) Nothing in my life has touched me more than the reception I've been greeted with today.

An appreciative murmur from the group. Rupert is uncomfortably close. He smiles and bows

Rupert (*oily*) Your Majesty.
Rassendyll (*grateful for Rupert's apparent credulity*) Thank you.

Rupert retreats to Michael. Flavia takes Rassendyll a little aside

Michael (*quietly furious*) Rupert! Ride like the devil to Zenda. Find
out what's gone wrong.
Rupert Your Royal Highness—I am already there.

Rupert slips easily away

Flavia (*confidentially*) Did you notice Michael?
Rassendyll Yes.
Flavia Before you arrived he was intolerable. Offensively intimate.
As though he were to be crowned, not you. When you arrived, he
seemed amazed. Struck dumb.
Rassendyll Nervous.
Flavia Dangerous. You must take care.
Rassendyll I will. (*A beat*) Of you as well.
Flavia What did you say?
Rassendyll Of you as well.
Flavia (*astonished*) I must be over-wrought. I thought you said . . .
Rassendyll I did.
Flavia You did. Well . . . thank you.
Rassendyll You'll have to help me.
Flavia (*faintly*) Yes. Yes, of course.
Rassendyll If you want to . . .
Flavia (*to cover her confusion*) Shall we go? I think it's time . . .
Rassendyll (*solicitously*) Are you ready?
Flavia I am . . . thank you.
Rassendyll (*to Sapt, with a new confidence*) Colonel Sapt? Shall we
proceed?
Sapt Of course. (*To the others*) Gentlemen, your Royal Highness.

*And the group turn together to face out front. Lights come up on them as
though the doors had opened. Music:* La Générosité *from Twelve
Marches by Telemann. A huge roar of applause. Cheers, bells. Petals
fall from above and flutter down amongst the group. Flavia smiles
encouragement at Rassendyll, who turns and waves to the crowd. For
Sapt, Fritz and Rassendyll a mood of relief and nervous excitement*

The Lights burn ever more brightly and then suddenly dim to black-out

ACT II

SCENE 1

The Coronation Ball. Later that evening

A wide and pleasant verandah. Tall french windows allow a glimpse of the lighted ballroom beyond. Coloured lanterns and candlelight outside. A full moon. Couples wander to and fro. A waltz is playing. We hear distant ballroom chatter

Fritz and Sapt stroll onto the verandah

Sapt So far, so good.

Fritz One or two difficult moments.

Sapt He keeps bowing to people. He's supposed to be the King!

Fritz I didn't show him how to dance the Pivaky.

Sapt His guesswork was inspired.

Fritz Look out! Here he comes with the Prince of Wales!

Rassendyll enters with the future Edward VII. His toughest challenge yet. He is overawed—but must treat Edward as a cousin

Rassendyll It is a matter of the utmost regret to me and to all the people of our country that Her Majesty Queen Victoria has been unable to accompany your Royal Highness, and be present at this, perhaps the most important . . .

Edward Frankly, old man it's good to be away from her. I managed to persuade the old girl not to come. Packed her off to Scotland!

Rassendyll We trust Her Majesty enjoys good health and that the many affairs of state proceeding from so great an Empire . . .

Edward Strong as a horse. She'll see me out. Ah, Sapt!

Sapt Your Royal Highness.

Edward (*proffering an unlit cigar*) Does anybody have a light?

Fritz Sir. (*He lights the Prince's cigar*)

Edward Talking of horses—shall we be racing tomorrow?

Rassendyll By all means . . .

Sapt and Fritz react. Racing is quite out of the question

Rassendyll (*improvising*) Except that all the royal horses . . . (*He looks to Fritz for help*)

Fritz . . . have to be shod . . .

Edward SHOT?

Sapt SHOD!!

Edward And I'm missing Cheltenham to be here. Mr Dorkins' my favourite for the three-thirty.

Rassendyll He had a very good season last year.

Edward Yes, yes, indeed. Dazzling speed. A remarkable performance at Newmarket in the Breeders Cup.

Rassendyll That was a splendid race! Do you remember how he appeared on Shoemaker's outside in the final furlong and showed the lot of them a clean pair of heels . . .

Prince Rudolph couldn't know this. Fritz and Sapt tense, Edward is puzzled. Rassendyll realises he's gone too far

Edward You speak as though you were there, old man.

Sapt (*trying to change the subject*) I trust your Royal Highness and his party are comfortably accommodated?

Edward Perfectly. (*Turning back to Rassendyll*) But——you haven't been in England since you were a child.

Rassendyll No. . . .

Edward You've come a long way.

Rassendyll (*heartfelt*) Further than you think.

Edward Altogether splendid coronation.

Rassendyll Thank you.

Edward Well, you can come and have a good laugh at mine—if I ever get there. Probably have to be wheeled in.

They all laugh

Where's that devil Carrington? He promised me an introduction to the lovely Helga Von Strofzin. Excuse me, dear fellow . . .

Fritz is horrified. Helga is his beloved

Edward goes

Rassendyll breathes a sigh of relief

Sapt A word your Majesty. Beside the door, the Arch-Duchess Louise . . .
Rassendyll Which?
Sapt The creature in the red silk.
Fritz And you see those feathers . . .
Rassendyll Yes . . .
Fritz That's your aunt. The Princess Alicia.
Sapt And the fellow in the green shako is Von Doosenburg—the Prussian Ambassador.
Fritz Clever fellow . . .
Sapt Careful what you say to him.
Fritz Particularly about the Danube.
Sapt (*impatiently*) The *ELBE* . . .
Fritz Look out! The Princess.

Flavia floats onto the balcony—dressed in a beautiful white evening gown

Flavia They're about to play another waltz . . .
Rassendyll It would be a *great* relief.

The orchestra strikes up, and they dance—very well. As they dance, the dialogue continues

This is such fun. I can't begin to tell you.
Flavia Where did you learn to dance your Majesty?
Rassendyll (*inspired*) Mother taught me.
Flavia (*after a moment*) She died when you were two.
Rassendyll (*clinging on*) The thought of her inspires me . . .
Flavia The last time we danced—you very nearly fractured my toe.
Rassendyll (*simply*) I've turned over a new leaf.
Flavia You have, you have . . .

The music ends. They turn to Sapt and Fritz

Sapt Your Royal Highness looks pretty as a picture.
Flavia What picture did you have in mind Colonel?
Fritz One lovelier than any hanging in this palace, Ma'am.
Flavia That simply isn't true. But you're gallant to believe it Fritz. Oh, I think Helga von Strofzin needs to be rescued from the English Ambassador. What's his name?
Rassendyll (*a trifle too promptly*) Drummond. He's a terrible bore. Rumour has it that he once became so tedious over dinner that his

wife—poor thing—fell asleep in her sorbet. His club has issued a
warning . . .
Sapt (*softly*) Careful . . .
Flavia How do you know all this?
Rassendyll (*inspired*) The Prince of Wales told me!
Fritz (*impressed*) Very good.
Flavia You'd better get to poor Helga, before she passes away . . .
Fritz Ma'am.

Fritz clicks his heels, bows and makes a delighted exit

Rassendyll (*hinting*) Thank you Sapt.
Sapt (*impervious*) What for?
Rassendyll We're doing very well, thank you.
Sapt (*settling*) Splendid.
Flavia Would you be a good friend, Colonel Sapt, and find my wrap.
The night air is suddenly cold after the heat of that room . . .
Sapt Ah. Well, yes of course, your Majesty. (*Subtlety eludes him*)
Careful now.

Sapt goes

Rassendyll He thinks we should be careful . . .
Flavia How strange of him.
Rassendyll I can't think what he means . . .
Flavia You are very different tonight.
Rassendyll NO!—I mean . . . no.
Flavia You haven't said anything about Lilly.
Rassendyll (*stumped*) Lilly?
Flavia You moved her bed into your room.
Rassendyll (*improvising*) I thought it was the best thing to do. But
now I'll tell her—enough's enough!
Flavia I don't mind at all.
Rassendyll (*astonished*) How splendid of you!
Flavia How many did she have?
Rassendyll How many?
Flavia Puppies.
Rassendyll Puppies?? (*Light suddenly dawns*) OH—*puppies* . . . yes,
well—*lots.*
Flavia Good.
Rassendyll Lilly—yes—*dog*—of course. Dear old Lilly . . .
Flavia And what about the Prince of Wales?

Rassendyll (*confidently*) Back to the kennels with him!

Flavia (*taken aback*) Your Majesty!

Rassendyll No. You can't let any of them rule your life. You have to make it clear who's master . . . (*suddenly realisation*) . . . The Prince of Wales. Yes. Well. You have to keep these English on a tight lead. Don't you . . .

Flavia (*laughing*) You're very—amusing tonight.

Rassendyll I feel like an idiot. (*A beat*) I'm so glad you're here.

Flavia Thank you. I had to come.

Rassendyll Of course.

Flavia Might I say . . . how very much I appreciate . . . your kindness to me this evening. If we were always as we are tonight—what a future for us both.

Rassendyll I am overwhelmed.

Flavia I'd given up looking for you, but suddenly—here you are. My old friend. How strange it is to meet you like this.

Rassendyll No, no, I AM Rudolph. The person that I always was.

Flavia Your very face is thinner!

Rassendyll (*heartfelt*) Anxiety!

Flavia You mean about Michael.

Rassendyll He never liked me.

Flavia Nobody ever liked him—you know that. I tried to for a while, but that was a mistake.

Rassendyll Why?

Flavia You KNOW. He gawps at me. He creeps up behind garden walls and watches me. Sometimes if I'm out riding, I jump over a fence, and there he is—sitting on the other side. It's unnerving!

Rassendyll Of course.

Flavia I wish he'd leave me alone.

Rassendyll I can't tell you how he's interfered with *my* plans . . .

Flavia Now that you're crowned—take steps. As Colonel Sapt says—you really must be careful.

Rassendyll I'll do my best.

Flavia It was wise of you not to stay at Zenda.

Rassendyll Oh, certainly. A gloomy place . . .

A moment passes

Flavia People still think we're going to be married, don't they?

Rassendyll Ah.

Flavia Marshal Strakencz says it will secure the future of the

Kingdom. My family has many friends in the north. If they see us married, it will check their doubts . . .

Rassendyll I understand.

Flavia I can accept any conditions you would like to set. Separate apartments, separate responsibilities. A distance.

Rassendyll (*passionately*) NO! No. Why should we? Why should we be kept apart?

Flavia This is a different tone of voice.

Rassendyll I have a very different point of view . . .

Flavia (*a moment*) Why have you changed towards me?

Rassendyll Ah . . .

Flavia The last time we met . . .

Rassendyll (*anxiously*) Yes?

Flavia I cried for a day afterwards.

Rassendyll The monster.

Flavia What?

Rassendyll (*hastily*) I was rude . . .?

Flavia Yes, very . . . Rather childish.

Rassendyll Not any more.

Flavia Can I believe you?

Rassendyll (*carefully*) When I walked into the cathedral, I saw you for the first time. You put out a hand to help me and I was so grateful. Nothing in my life had prepared me for that moment. Now I want to be honest with you. And I'm afraid it's the one thing that will prove impossible.

Flavia Don't say that. Why?

Rassendyll Events will overtake us.

Flavia I don't understand.

Rassendyll I love you. That's the truth. I swear it.

Distant music

Flavia (*astonished*) I believe you.

Rassendyll In the Cathedral—when we met—I suddenly felt such calm. In the middle of all that noise—I knew my first real moment of peace. Other voices stopped nagging at me. My life changed.

Flavia Yes.

Rassendyll And you?

Flavia I don't know.

Rassendyll Of course.

Flavia I feel confused. (*Long beat. She moves away from him a little—*

concentrating) You know—all last month it rained. Grey skies, mist, fog, ugly dull mornings. I was at Falkenberg. The forest seemed to be full of smoke—not that we could see much of it, the clouds were so low. On the last day of the month, I opened the shutters of my window early—before anyone else was stirring—and the bad weather had vanished completely. I felt warm light on my skin and the world outside reared up before me like a regiment of cavalry—ready for anything. It was wonderful. Wonderful. Where had it been? What should I do now? How could I do justice to it? The old housekeeper found me in tears. And you see. I'm crying again.

Rassendyll (*softly*) If we were to dance—no-one would notice.

And they do

A moment later Antoinette de Mauban, looking beautiful and pale, appears at the door. She watches them for a moment

Rassendyll (*involuntarily*) Madame de Mauban!

Antoinette I don't believe we've met, your Majesty. (*She curtsies deeply*)

Flavia (*slightly puzzled*) But you know her . . .

Rassendyll Yes. No. I've *seen* her.

Flavia (*bowing slightly to her*) Madame.

Antoinette Your Royal Highness.

Flavia How I've always longed to meet you.

Antoinette Yes, of course.

Flavia You are Duke Michael's guest?

Antoinette That's one way of describing it . . .

Flavia He is fortunate to have so beautiful a companion.

Antoinette (*laughing*) Elle rougit sous le compliment.

Rassendyll Where IS Duke Michael?

Antoinette Vanished without trace. I'm used to it, your Majesty. He's always disappearing. He thinks it makes me eager to pursue him.

Flavia Michael is very diligent, Madame.

Antoinette To you perhaps.

Flavia It is his natural disposition.

Antoinette Really? Well, I'm pleased to hear it. He keeps it well hidden from me.

Rassendyll Can we be of any service to you?

Antoinette Not yet. (*A beat*) Your Majesty has been hunting?

Rassendyll (*nervously*) Yes.

Antoinette The Rattenspitze Falls are most impressive. Did you get to see them?

Rassendyll No. I didn't go . . . WE didn't go in that direction.

Antoinette But of course—you know them well.

Sapt suddenly arrives

Sapt Your Majesty—a word. Forgive us, Ma'am. (*A scowl in the direction of Antoinette*)

Flavia Of course.

Rassendyll and Sapt move away

Sapt You know who that woman is?

Rassendyll I do. I rather fear she knows who I am too.

Sapt Does she indeed? All the more reason to be on our way. Michael was seen leaving the city as though all the devils in hell were after him. It's nearly ten. We should be on our way.

Rassendyll Already?

Sapt Yes, lad. It's time.

Rassendyll (*anguished*) Oh no . . .

Sapt Have you forgotten, Rassendyll—the King! I won't feel easy till I'm back with him and you're a cloud of dust on the other side of the German border. Make your farewells. I hope you weren't too nice to her.

Rassendyll Oh God.

Fritz von Tarlenheim appears at the door, very much part of a secret plot

Fritz Urgent business, your Majesty. Affairs of state. (*Significantly*) It's possible they'll keep you busy for an hour. MAYBE TWO . . .

Sapt All right, all right Fritz. We get the point. Your Majesty . . .

Rassendyll (*to Flavia*) I have to go.

Flavia Of course. Is everything all right?

Rassendyll No. Yes. Only that I've got to leave you.

Flavia We'll meet tomorrow.

Rassendyll God willing.

Flavia For heaven's sake—don't doubt it for a moment.

Rassendyll Remember what we've said.

Flavia Always.

Rassendyll Can you believe me?

Flavia Yes—oh yes.

Rassendyll (*seizing her hand and kissing it. Greatly upset*) Good night. Good night.

And he goes. Sapt and Fritz follow

Flavia (*puzzled at his distress*) Good night.

A pause

Antoinette Are you in love, your Royal Highness?

Flavia (*faintly*) Yes.

Antoinette (*momentarily concerned*) I thought so. Well. Be careful.

Flavia You're the second person who's said that to me this evening.

Antoinette There's a carriage waiting for me. Great black wagon. Like something out of a nightmare. I leave for Zenda tonight.

Flavia Have a safe journey.

Antoinette (*brightly*) It will be intolerable. Good night, your Royal Highness.

Flavia Good night, Madame.

And the scene fades in a thunder of horses' hooves and carriage wheels

SCENE 2

The Hunting Lodge. Darkness. Moonlight

Sapt and Rassendyll emerge, exhausted from the journey. They pause outside

Sapt Two hours from the Palace. Good. Catch your breath. Then— inside, relieve Old Josef and we go our separate ways. Pray God Fritz has played his part.

Rassendyll My reign is over.

Sapt Ha! King for twelve hours. More than enough.

Rassendyll Wait a moment, Sapt.

Sapt What now?

Rassendyll She was not in the least what I'd expected.

Sapt Who?

Rassendyll The Princess Flavia. Curious. I thought she'd be a puppet. Pretty, painted, exquisitely finished.

Sapt Wasn't she?
Rassendyll No. She was quite different. You should have warned me.
Sapt What about?
Rassendyll Sapt, I'll miss her very much. I could tolerate a king's life for more than just a dozen hours you see.

An odd moment. Sapt looks at him curiously

Sapt Don't, Rassendyll. Don't look down the wrong road.
Rassendyll No. I won't. (*A beat*) But I've wooed her for the King. I hope he's pleased. Come on. Let's hurry.

And they advance into the darkened room. The clock ticks

Sapt No lights. Odd.
Rassendyll It could be a precaution.
Sapt I don't like it.
Rassendyll Where's Josef?
Sapt (*faintly*) Where's the King?
Rassendyll Sapt! What's the matter?
Sapt Something's wrong. I can smell it. We've blundered, boy.
Rassendyll Calm yourself!
Sapt I can't get my breath. Suppose that Michael . . .
Rassendyll I've got some matches . . . (*a moment passes*) Aahh!! Damnation take it!
Sapt Rassendyll!
Rassendyll I slipped. The floor's wet . . . What the devil . . .
Sapt Are you hurt?

Silence

Rassendyll! Rassendyll!!
Rassendyll Dear God, it's blood.
Sapt NO!

In the half light we see Rassendyll fumble with the box of matches. Suddenly a match flares. We see Josef sitting at a table, his throat cut, blood everywhere. He's very close to Rassendyll—who gasps, drops the match, staggers back

Rassendyll It's Josef. He's dead. His throat's cut.
Sapt The King. Dear God—the King . . .

Another match. This time Rassendyll attaches the flame to a candle, which splutters into life

Hurry. Please. The cellar. I made a bed for him in the cellar. Through the trap door. Quickly man!

Rassendyll (*trying the trap door*) Damn me—it's heavy . . . There!

Rassendyll disappears down below the floor

The clock ticks. Seconds pass

Sapt Dear God . . . We did our best. It seemed the only way . . .

Rassendyll returns, sombre

Rassendyll He's not there. The King's not there.

Sapt staggers. Rassendyll rushes to support him

Easy, easy. Sit here. Look—drink this. I'll put Josef on the King's bed. (*He drags Josef to the trapdoor*) Poor chap. I think he put up quite a fight . . .

Rassendyll drags Josef down the stairs, and a few seconds later returns

Rassendyll and Sapt sit by the table

Sapt They've got our King. Michael's creatures came prowling. Michael will know our secret by now. He left Strelsau long before we did. I can guess where he went.

Rassendyll Zenda?

Sapt Where else?

Rassendyll And the King?

Sapt Zenda too. Or in his grave.

Rassendyll They wouldn't dare.

Sapt Oh yes they would. (*A sudden thought strikes him*) But now they've seen you—they'll keep him alive. I *know* it. And while you're alive—we've got Michael in check. However he plays the game—we've got him in check. We just keep moving you around the board.

Rassendyll (*incredulous*) What do you mean?

Sapt Back to your pretty queen.

Rassendyll Me? Go back?

Sapt Yes. The King must be in Strelsau again tomorrow.

Rassendyll The King?

Sapt He that was *crowned* King.

Rassendyll No. NO! We must go back to Strelsau and tell the truth.
Then rouse the city and lay siege to Zenda.

Sapt (*with some impatience*) Tell the Bishop and the Marshal and the
people of the city that they crowned the wrong man? Oh—but it
doesn't matter. We only did it because the REAL king was flat on
his back with a bottle screwed in his mouth!!

Rassendyll They'll find me out.

Sapt Not you, Rassendyll. Dear God man, we need you now more
than ever. And think—how can they denounce you without
denouncing themselves?—"This is not the King, because we
kidnapped the King and murdered his servant." Can they say that?

Rassendyll No. It's true. They're caught as well. (*Suddenly*) But
Flavia. That won't be quite so easy.

Sapt No. I can see that now.

A beat

Rassendyll Sapt—I'll try it.

Sapt Yes!

Rassendyll Let's see it through.

Sapt God bless you, boy. Well played. NOW—back to the horses
. . . WAIT! What was that . . . I heard something . . .

Rassendyll Yes, footsteps.

Sapt Quick—the candle.

Rassendyll extinguishes it

They won't be expecting us. Michael's sent them back to clear up
the mess. Can you defend yourself?

Rassendyll Sabre and foil at Eton, Sapt. Played for the Varsity.

Sapt (*contemptuously*) See what you can do with this . . . (*He hands
him a huge ancient sabre*) I've a revolver.

Rassendyll Shh! Hide over there . . . I'll give them a surprise. (*He
places himself where Josef was slumped*)

*The light of two bullseye lanterns flashes across the stage. Two men
move into the room: Detchard: a thin-faced, cruel hitman; and
Bersonin: a chubby, oily Belgian*

Detchard I don't usually have to bury the people I kill.

Bersonin So—the Duke says we are careless, that we have to do a
little housework. Mama always told me to leave the kitchen clean
and tidy . . .

Detchard Let's get on with it. He's over there.

They move to either side of the body

Bersonin Where shall we put him? Outside? Under a tree? Under the floorboards?

Detchard Cut him up. Drop his bits down the well.

Rassendyll Actually, I have a place reserved in the family tomb.

Bersonin Really?—AAAAAHHH!!

And all hell breaks loose. The table goes flying, lantern beams flash, Rassendyll lays into Detchard with the sabre, Sapt fires the revolver and wounds Detchard—who curses and stumbles. Sapt makes for the door, Detchard pushes him back. A struggle ensues. Finally, Detchard and Bersonin are left fighting each other

Sapt and Rassendyll sneak away

Through all this we hear a spirited gypsy tune

From outside we hear Rassendyll and Sapt

Rassendyll Delighted to have made your acquaintance, gentlemen!

Sapt (*as he prepares to fire another shot back into the house*) God save the King!!

And the shot rings out, as the gypsy music swells to a triumphant, strutting celebration of their victory. The scene changes to . . .

SCENE 3

Zenda

We see Rupert dancing, bottle in hand, to the gypsy tune. As it fades he throws himself into a deep armchair. Antoinette watches him

Antoinette I really don't like you, Rupert. I'm a connoisseur of unpleasant men—so I know what I'm talking about.

Rupert I can see that you're impressed . . .

Antoinette Rats have a more coherent morality.

Rupert I swear on my mother's grave—we have no wish to kill him.

Antoinette Only to lock him up, deprive him of food and light, and chain him to the floor like an animal. A liberal regime . . .

Rupert Apparently it's necessary.

Antoinette Why does Michael allow it? Why won't he see me?

Rupert He's busy.

Antoinette But you've botched it, haven't you? The King's been crowned in Strelsau. You saw it yourself. Two nights ago I watched him dancing . . .

Rupert The play actor.

Antoinette I wouldn't patronise him. He's outwitted you.

Rupert I'd love to kiss you.

Antoinette I've already washed.

Rupert You're intrigued aren't you? A creature of the night—drawn in by the flicker of conspiracy.

Antoinette Tell Michael that I need to see him. If I don't—I'll leave.

Rupert I'm not sure if that's possible.

Antoinette The schoolyard bully . . .

Rupert It's nice of you to help us.

Antoinette Help *you*?! Listen. What I did, I did for Michael. . . *do* for Michael.

Rupert Good.

Antoinette He sees the weakness of the King. The generals will support him . . .

Rupert You know how dangerous he is. Cruel.

Antoinette If I can help, I will. But still it's odd that he won't see me.

Rupert He takes a pleasure in severity which even startles me.

Antoinette There's been a change here. Footsteps in the middle of the night, candles still burning after dawn . . .

Rupert Perhaps you're not aware of what goes on behind his door some nights.

Antoinette Keep your secrets to yourself. They're of no use to me.

Rupert If it were up to me, King Rudolph would be sharing my apartments. Feather bed, roast beef, a nice big window, proper toilet facilities . . .

Antoinette Then why don't you *do* something about it?

Rupert Security. Michael's instructions. He likes to gloat.

Antoinette Oh God.

A pause

Rupert We could adapt a little.

Antoinette What?

Rupert Examine our position.

Antoinette How?

Rupert Visit the play actor. Put a proposition to him.

Antoinette Betray the Duke.

Rupert Let's say we'd contemplate a different strategy.

Antoinette Go on.

Rupert The play actor sits on the throne. Everybody thinks he's King. We know he's not. I'm sure he'd like us to keep quiet about it. Michael on the other hand has a hard game ahead of him . . .

Antoinette So stick a dagger in his back, tip his body in the moat . . .

Rupert And go to live in Strelsau. Where everybody goes to bed at nine. Even the rats.

Antoinette You revolt me.

Rupert Yes. But nonetheless . . .

Antoinette No. NO!

Rupert You're stubborn.

Antoinette Michael had a plan. Order through strength. It made sense. I understood what he was getting at. *He has a vision.* You just want to strut from bed to bed—leaving a string of mistresses with ruined lives and handsome little bastards . . .

Rupert I do admire you.

Suddenly a curtain twitches. Michael appears from behind it. A smug, bitter look about him

Michael That's enough. I've made my point. We trust her.

Antoinette (*staggered*) Michael . . .

Michael Don't distress yourself, my dear. We needed to find out exactly how reliable you were.

Antoinette Michael.

Michael And you passed with flying colours. Rupert here was confident he'd have you promising to ditch me within minutes.

Rupert (*dryly*) Very impressive.

Michael (*to Rupert*) How you enjoyed yourself, you nasty child. Stirring up dirt.

Rupert And knowing that you had to listen. It was fun.

Michael Fortunately Antoinette knows better than to trust you. Let alone believe you.

Antoinette How could you Michael . . .?

Michael Don't be sentimental, Madame. We are playing for the highest stakes. I'm fond of you. That doesn't mean I trust you. Does it?

Antoinette You let this creature test me while you WATCHED . . .

Rupert He likes to watch . . .

Michael Be quiet or I'll make you quiet.

Antoinette You should have known . . . you could have trusted *me*.

Michael Yes, yes. Perhaps. Now. We must use you, Madame—to facilitate a plan. I need hardly say how delicate the matter is. You have to write a letter to the King. I mean the King in Strelsau.

Rupert Sapt won't let him see it.

Michael Very well. A letter to the Princess then. You amused us yesterday with tales of how in love they seemed to be with one another. She'll pass on a warning to him. Maybe we can make her jealous too.

Rupert A letter from another woman. Good.

Michael Loosen his hold on her . . .

Rupert So Flavia can turn to you.

Antoinette That's not true! Michael. Tell him.

Sinister music. The Lights flicker

Michael Be very careful, Rupert. (*A beat*) Now, Madame—shall we go in and write?

Michael escorts Antoinette to the door

The music—stealthy, evil—creeps up on the light and smothers it

SCENE 4

The Palace

Rassendyll and Fritz are looking through a huge old photograph album. Sapt is standing nearby

Fritz And *this* one is your great-uncle. He's called Adolf. Your maternal grandmother's half-brother. Reclusive. Wrote a book about cooking—"A Duke's Diet". Married to a Romanoff—Astrid-Eugenie . . .

Rassendyll (*desperately*) It's no good. I can't remember any of this. They all look the same.

Sapt Necessary homework. They mustn't catch you out.

Rassendyll Of course. But how long are we going to wait?

Sapt It's only been two days.

Fritz And you're doing splendidly. Introducing General Wintenberg and his wife to one another. People seemed to think you were being funny . . .

Sapt (*seriously*) You handled the border negotiations well. No-one could have managed the affair better. You'd read the papers.

Rassendyll I enjoyed that . . . *understood* it. I knew what to do.

Fritz Jolly good.

Rassendyll Don't leave me here too long.

Sapt We'll see you safely home.

Rassendyll I could begin to think this was my destiny . . .

An uneasy moment

Sapt Careful, lad . . .

Rassendyll At the first opportunity, we must make our move against Michael. I shall give orders . . .

Sapt Rassendyll!!

Rassendyll (*sharply*) Who dares resist me?

A moment

Fritz We're in your hands.

Rassendyll Are we certain that the King's at Zenda?

Sapt We've bribed one of Michael's servants. There is a prisoner—he can't discover who, and we'll not tell him—kept in the Castle dungeons. Only Michael's special henchmen guard him—Hentzau, Detchard, Bersonin . . .

Rassendyll We'll bring this to a head. I'll rescue him. I must. You Sapt, and Fritz, have far too much to lose. I can afford to disappear.

Sapt Nothing hasty now.

Rassendyll Sapt! I could delay for ever. DON'T YOU UNDERSTAND? I feel that I've come home. I recognise myself. How can I make you see? I talk to these ambassadors and officers of state—and feel at ease.

Sapt Well. You're an honourable man.

Rassendyll Honour's all that I'll be left with.

Sapt What do you mean by that?

Rassendyll When I've gone.

Sapt But you will go . . .

Rassendyll Oh yes. (*A long moment*) I will.

Fritz tries to change the subject

Fritz Why don't we simply storm the castle? There's no garrison to speak of there. I know some splendid fellows who . . .

Sapt (*impatiently*) NO. NO. The first sign of trouble and they'd kill the King. Spirit his body through some secret passage—only to re-appear with it as proof that *we're* the villains.

Fritz Do you really think so?

Rassendyll It's a brave thought, Fritz.

Sapt But a stupid one.

Suddenly the Princess Flavia appears. Fritz and Sapt are surprised—Rassendyll delighted

Flavia (*agitated*) Gentlemen.

A beat

I have received a letter.

Rassendyll Yes?

Flavia I think you ought to see it.

Sapt (*alarmed*) No!

Rassendyll Show it to me.

Flavia Here. It concerns your safety.

Fritz (*inspired by Sapt's alarm*) Don't believe it!

Flavia What?

Fritz It's an absurd accusation. Can't you see they're desperate . . .

Sapt Be quiet, Fritz!

Fritz Just a thought.

Flavia It contains no accusation.

Fritz (*hopelessly*) There you are then!

Rassendyll Sapt—look at this. (*He hands the note to Sapt*)

Sapt (*reading*) "The King is in danger. Tell him this. At the end of the Old Avenue there stands a house in large grounds. There is a gate in the wall at the back. At twelve tonight, the King should enter alone by that gate and walk to the old laundry behind the house. There he will find someone who will tell him what most dearly touches his life and throne. This is written by a woman that loves him, an unhappy woman whose name begins with 'A' . . ."

Fritz I don't remember a gate in that wall. Surely . . .

Sapt For heaven's sake . . .!

Fritz There's a little wrought iron affair on the Royal Avenue . . .

Sapt Shut up and think! Or try to. 'A' . . .
Rassendyll Antoinette de Mauban.
Fritz No!
Sapt (*grimly*) Very good.
Flavia (*distantly*) A woman that loves him . . .
Rassendyll NO! *Please.* Don't think that.
Sapt It's not from her.
Flavia What?
Sapt Black Michael wrote that latter. It's a trap.
Fritz (*keeping up*) Of *course.*
Flavia What's going on? I have a right to know.
Sapt Plots and treachery, my dear, nothing unusual. Leave it to me.
   I'll put a troop of men inside that wash house tonight . . .
Rassendyll No. Though the letter was dictated by Black Michael—it
   comes from Antoinette de Mauban. I feel sure that we can trust her.
Sapt Never!
Rassendyll She could be useful to us.
Sapt No!
Rassendyll Trust me, Sapt. I'll turn this trick to our advantage.
Sapt (*after a moment*) Very well. But I'll come with you.
Rassendyll No, you won't.
Sapt It makes no sense!
Rassendyll Leave it to me. I'll go.
Sapt (*forgetting Flavia*) The devil you will!

Flavia looks sharply at him. Even Sapt can't speak to a king like this

   If you'll forgive me saying so, your Majesty . . .
Rassendyll (*saving the day*) You forget yourself, Colonel Sapt. This
   matter concerns me—and I best know how to handle it.
Sapt (*accepting defeat*) Sir!
Flavia Why do you have to meet this woman who loves you? What
   dearly touches your life?
Rassendyll Gentlemen, please . . .

*Fritz and Sapt retreat to the very back of the gallery. Sapt strains to
hear the conversation*

Flavia Don't make me doubt you now.
Rassendyll I swear to you . . .
Flavia Why won't you tell me?
Rassendyll (*in agony*) I would . . . I will. But not yet.

Flavia (*flaring up*) You know her well. Madame de Mauban!

Rassendyll *No.*

Flavia You met abroad. She understood how lonely you felt. Now that you're crowned—she's come for her reward!

Rassendyll You're *wrong!* I met her once. On a station platform. At Dresden. We spoke for thirty seconds. That's God's truth. I wouldn't. . . . I *couldn't* lie to you.

Flavia But you're hiding something.

Rassendyll Yes . . .

Flavia I'm suddenly afraid that I might lose you . . . that I might be left alone again.

Rassendyll Don't talk like that. I love you. More than life or truth or honour.

Flavia Then tell me why you're going.

Rassendyll Oh—if I were not the King. Then I could tell you.

Flavia If you were not the King?

Rassendyll Then it would be simple.

Flavia Why should it matter to me what you are?

Rassendyll What?

Flavia If you were a beggar on the streets of Strelsau I would love you—tell you everything. Please. Trust me, Rudolph.

Rassendyll If I were just a private gentleman?

Flavia King, commoner . . . it's not important to me. Don't you understand?

Rassendyll Perhaps . . .

Flavia I love you. Nothing can change that. Nothing.

Rassendyll Dear God.

Flavia But please—I beg of you. Hide nothing from me.

Rassendyll Then perhaps there's hope.

Flavia Tell me.

Rassendyll Flavia you're right. I'll tell you—trust you utterly . . .

Flavia Yes!

From the end of the gallery comes Sapt's voice—loud and threatening

Sapt Your Majesty! We have no time to lose!

Rassendyll I'm not . . .

Sapt (*suddenly there*) Take care your Majesty. Perils surround us. To protect the King—I'd put a bullet in my closest friend.

Rassendyll I think you would.

Flavia Rudolph! Tell me. Quickly, before you go.

Sapt No! As you love the King, your Royal Highness, ask no more questions.

Flavia This is cruel, Colonel Sapt.

Sapt Honour demands the King's silence.

Rassendyll Have you left me any honour?

Sapt Your Majesty . . .

Flavia No, Rudolph. Let him answer *me*. I've known you since I was a child, Colonel Sapt. You know I'd trust you with my life. You understand a great deal more than you'll admit—although of course you tell us otherwise, and say you're only interested in battlefields or treaties. I think you understand my feelings for the King. Tell me . . . When shall I see him next?

A moment passes

Sapt (*deeply moved*) I cannot say, your Royal Highness.

Flavia Rudolph?

Silence

Fritz?

Silence. A moment passes

Well then—good night. (*A beat*) You could have trusted me.

Flavia goes

Rassendyll I didn't expect this.

Sapt No.

Rassendyll It wasn't part of our bargain.

Sapt No. Of course not.

Rassendyll Will she ever forgive me?

Sapt (*after a moment*) It's nearly time.

Rassendyll Bright hopes dim. I know what I must do.

Sapt (*softly*) You're the finest Elphberg of them all.

Rassendyll I'd better hurry.

The Lights fade. Music swells

SCENE 5

The Old Laundry

Darkness, moonlight. Racks of cloths and linen drying. Vats of water.
Washing boards, lines, blocks of soap. Rupert, Detchard and Bersonin
are hidden. Rassendyll—sword drawn—makes his way through the
clutter. Suddenly—a flurry of skirt and cloak as Antoinette appears

Antoinette Did you close the door?
Rassendyll Yes.
Antoinette We've little time. I know you, Mr Rassendyll. We met at
    Dresden.
Rassendyll I don't think so.
Antoinette Don't waste time persuading me that you're the king. I
    wrote that letter on the Duke's orders.
Rassendyll I know.
Antoinette (*amused*) We are alone, Mr Rassendyll.
Rassendyll (*believing her*) Yes.
Antoinette But in five minutes Rupert of Hentzau will be here with
    two of his friends. They mean to kill you.
Rassendyll Or be killed.
Antoinette No tiresome heroics, please. Just listen. The King is ill. If
    he's not rescued—he may die. When you're killed your body will be
    used to compromise your friends. Michael will arrest Sapt and the
    others—and proclaim a state of siege in Strelsau. Then he'll
    despatch a messenger to Zenda. Rupert will kill the King—and
    Michael will declare himself regent . . .
Rassendyll And you?
Antoinette (*bitterly*) I'll be abandoned—I can see that now. I'm
    Michael's instrument. I used to think that I was something more.
    Perhaps if the King is rescued—I can run away with him. (*A beat*)
    You see—I never learn. It's quite a failing.
Rassendyll How do I get into Zenda?
Antoinette Come with me as my driver.
Rassendyll Good!
Antoinette You're his height and build. Meet me at the palace later.
    My instructions are to see you murdered, wait two hours—and
    then return to Zenda. Now *GO*. I'll say you never came . . .
Rassendyll Sh!! I can hear footsteps.

Antoinette Damn them, they're here too soon. Look. Through the window. What do you see?

Rassendyll Nothing.

Antoinette They're hiding. Waiting for me to go. Then they'll attack . . .

Rassendyll Three against one.

Antoinette What shall we do?

Rassendyll Exactly as they've planned. Good night, Madame. Wait for me at the Palace.

Antoinette You're very sure you'll get the better of them.

Rassendyll Yes. (*Beat*) I have a job to do.

Antoinette Good luck, Mr Rassendyll.

Rassendyll Thank you.

They shake hands excitedly

Music, tense underscore

Antoinette leaves

Rassendyll takes out his revolver. A few seconds pass

(*Shouting*) Good evening, Gentlemen!

Rupert (*startled, improvising*) I—I have an offer for you, Mr Rassendyll.

Rassendyll You're talking to the King.

Rupert (*laughing*) Of course. Your Majesty. We have an offer.

Rassendyll Tell me about it.

Rupert Shall we speak outside?

Rassendyll My hearing is very good. Tell me from where you are.

Rupert (*after a moment*) I will. It's a safe conduct to the frontier, and fifty thousand pounds.

Rassendyll A King's ransom.

Rupert Yes indeed.

Rassendyll Tempting, but—thank you—*no*. There's still so much of my kingdom that I have to see.

Rupert If you'll allow me to approach, I might be able to persuade you.

Rassendyll I have a clear view of you, gentlemen. Rupert of Hentzau may come closer, but he MUST be unaccompanied . . .

Rupert advances until we can see him

Rupert (*softly*) I have another proposition.

Rassendyll A generous one I hope.

Rupert Attack Zenda boldly. Let Sapt and Tarlenheim lead.

Rassendyll Go on.

Rupert Arrange the time with me . . .

Rassendyll I'll take the details later, do you mind?

Rupert Sapt and Fritz will fall. Michael will fall . . .

Rassendyll Michael?

Rupert Like the dog he is. The prisoner—our "other" king—will go by secret passages to hell. Two men will be left—I, Rupert Hentzau, and you—the King of Ruritania. Isn't that a hand to play? A throne and your princess! And then for me—Michael's estates and your eternal gratitude.

Rassendyll While you're above ground hell lacks a master.

Rupert Don't be too hard on me—"your Majesty". For tuppence I'd relieve you of the Princess Flavia. So fresh and handsome. You're a lucky man. Quick off the mark. I'll wager the next Elphberg will be red enough for all that Michael may be called his father . . .

Rassendyll Damn you!

Rupert (*protesting*) Oh your Majesty . . .

A beat

Rassendyll Let your friends approach. We need to settle details.

Rupert Of course. (*Shouting*) Detchard! Bersonin!

The other two approach

Rassendyll Come in, please.

The three villains come up into the darkness of the laundry room

Rassendyll is lurking behind a clothes-line festooned with sheets

Does Mr Detchard have the fifty thousand pounds? I don't see it with him . . .

Rupert Come, Mr Rassendyll, we'd like to see you . . .

Rassendyll I'm sure you would.

Detchard I'll go and find him.

Rupert Take care.

Detchard I fear you'll make us stain this linen with your blood.

Bersonin And the Duke will want us to clear up again. I do hate washing, Mr Rassendyll . . .

Detchard lunges at the clothes-line Rassendyll is behind. The first part of the fight involves passes through the sheets: the villains' swords against Rassendyll's sword and long-handled mop. The fight then breaks into the open. Just as Rassendyll seems to be at their mercy, he disappears behind the sheets again. Rupert sends Detchard behind the sheets to get him. We hear a series of passes, then the sound of fisticuffs, then the sound of Detchard's body hitting the deck with a groan. Rupert sends the nervous Bersonin behind the sheets. He receives similar treatment. Rupert strolls to one end of the sheets, but just as he disappears behind them, Rassendyll appears round the other end. Rassendyll gets to a safe distance and waits. All three villains lunge back through the sheets at the same time. They are shocked to find that Rassendyll has escaped

Rassendyll (*at a safe distance*) Thank you gentlemen! Good night!
Rupert (*irritated but impressed*) I *say*!

Music swirls up as the Lights fade

SCENE 6

The Great Gallery at the Palace. Half-an-hour later

Candles, torches

Antoinette and Rassendyll are talking

Antoinette How does his jacket fit you, sire?
Rassendyll Not quite so well as his hat.
Antoinette The colours of his livery are hideous.
Rassendyll A good thing that it's dark, Madame.
Antoinette No-one of taste could bear to look at you.
Rassendyll So much the better.
Antoinette We must not be discovered.
Rassendyll Sapt and Fritz will follow us. When the King is safe I will let down the drawbridge.

Suddenly—a movement at one end of the gallery. A shadowy figure—Flavia—appears

Rassendyll and Antoinette don't notice her

Antoinette The time is nearly on us. We must leave at ten o'clock.

Rassendyll Courage, m'lady. It's a fine night for an adventure.

Antoinette Have you told the Princess?

Rassendyll Better that she doesn't know.

Antoinette When I first saw you I was quite convinced we'd end up in some scrape together.

Rassendyll You look as dauntless as you did that day.

Antoinette And you a little less well dressed. Though truth to tell— the driving cape may yet be à la mode . . .

Rassendyll And will you wish me luck?

Antoinette After tonight our lives will be forever changed.

Flavia (*quietly; out of the darkness*) Yes, yes. Forever changed.

Rassendyll (*immensely startled*) Flavia!

Flavia No more bright mornings . . .

Rassendyll What are you doing here?

Flavia I came to see you.

Rassendyll Flavia . . .

Flavia I trusted you. Stupid of me. Stupid. STUPID. I thought you'd changed. You seemed so different. Now I know.

Rassendyll What are you saying?

Flavia You were about to leave. Goodbye.

Rassendyll Please listen to me . . .

Flavia (*with a sudden intensity*) You told me that you loved me more than truth. I never thought to ask how much you valued *that.*

Rassendyll I love you. To hear you say I don't is insupportable.

Flavia How can you love me and betray me?

Antoinette Listen . . .

Flavia You were leaving.

Rassendyll Yes . . .

Flavia With her.

Rassendyll I was—but . . .

Flavia I don't think I can bear this.

Antoinette (*urgently, to Rassendyll*) Tell her! For God's sake—tell her.

Flavia No! Spare me that. I can imagine all I need to know.

Antoinette Your Royal Highness . . .

Flavia And I'll remember just how calm she is—almost impatient. Eager to be on her way . . .

Antoinette Listen you *fool.* I love Duke Michael—*loved* him.

Flavia Now you love a King!

Antoinette No!

Flavia You can climb no higher, Madame!
Antoinette (*taking control*) Listen to me. This man is *not* the King!
Rassendyll (*urgently*) NO! Don't . . .
Antoinette (*resolutely*) His name is Rudolph Rassendyll. You met
him for the first time at the coronation.
Flavia NO—I don't believe you. NO!
Antoinette Think back. How many moments did you wonder at the
change in him? How often did you marvel at his transformation?
One day—an oaf, a spoilt child, the next—a King.
Flavia That's true, of course—but . . .
Antoinette Well, the spoilt child is locked in Zenda—dying slowly,
abjectly—in chains. Michael's servants guard him. Mr Rassendyll,
your Royal Highness, is more faithful than you know, for he and I
were just about to free the King. (*Drily*) We had this mad idea that
we might rescue him. That's all. It's perfectly straightforward really.

A long silence—in the middle of which we hear sad music, far away

Rassendyll (*quietly; gravely*) Everything I said was true—and untrue.
When you said you'd love me if I weren't the King—I thought I
could survive the lies I'd had to tell. I thought I saw a tiny gap, just
big enough for both of us to get through.
Flavia (*faintly*) Rudolph Rassendyll.
Rassendyll I came to Ruritania by chance. The King was kidnapped.
I became the King.
Flavia They made you do it.
Rassendyll Michael made us do it.
Flavia Yes. (*A beat*) And now?
Rassendyll I am a private gentleman. I love a Princess and I will love
her until I die. A great nation stands on the brink of ruin. I must
help to keep it from the edge. I am an honourable man . . .
Flavia Called Rudolph Rassendyll. (*A beat*) And you must go.
Rassendyll Give me a sign.

Flavia takes the red rose pinned to her dress and gives it to him

Flavia You will rescue the King and I will have to marry him. If you
are successful—I will never see you again. If you are not—I'll meet
you soon enough in another place. But you have been faithful, and
my heart rejoices at that. Goodbye my love. May God go with
you. If you'd let me I'd come too: tie up my hair, borrow an old
pistol, let them know I have a score to settle . . .

Rassendyll That would be . . .

Flavia Ridiculous.

Rassendyll I shouldn't mind.

Flavia You look . . .

Rassendyll Ridiculous. I know. A clown.

Flavia Like a play—disguises, intrigue, lovers . . .

Rassendyll Funny from a distance.

Flavia Yes.

Antoinette We have to *go*.

Flavia Madame de Mauban—I am in your debt.

Antoinette No, not at all!

Flavia Forgive me.

Antoinette Yes. Yes, of course. (*A beat*) This is unusual. Nobody's ever asked me to forgive them. I'm usually the one on my knees. Goodbye, your Royal Highness.

Antoinette moves away

Rassendyll Goodbye.

Rassendyll and Flavia embrace

Goodbye, my only love.

Flavia Be careful. I'll wait for you.

Rassendyll Goodbye.

Rassendyll goes

SCENE 7

Zenda

Hooves galloping and the creak of carriage wheels. The noise of a drawbridge coming down, a gate scraping open. Horses whinny. The sound of hooves and wheels on a wooden bridge

Suddenly the flicker of a torch. Antoinette and Rassendyll

Antoinette Prince Rudolph's in the dungeons way below us. You'll not be challenged here inside the castle. Your livery protects you. Detchard and Bersonin guard the King. Good luck. I'm sure you'll

think of something clever. Englishmen are so resourceful. (*A beat*)
If you need me—I'll be in bed, reading the Bible . . .

A figure materialises next to them—Detchard

Rassendyll moves into the shadows

Detchard Your friend appeared to be expecting us.

Antoinette Why, Mr Detchard . . .

Detchard Three of us waiting for him. How did he know that we were there?

Antoinette Perhaps he heard you.

Detchard I think he heard *you*, Madame.

Antoinette Really—I don't know what you mean . . .

Detchard We have little time. The Duke must make his move within a day or everything is lost. You know that we could ill afford tonight's lack of success.

Antoinette I did exactly as Duke Michael asked me. If his minions are incompetent, that's hardly my affair.

Detchard Rupert is waiting for you. I'll tell him that you're here. He has some questions.

Antoinette I imagine that the Duke has questions for the three of *you*. You've been out-witted twice now—with the odds very much in your favour . . .

Detchard Perhaps you shouldn't have returned to Zenda, Madame. Our patience is running out. We may not be so civilized in future.

Antoinette Civilized! That's never been a failing of yours, Mr Detchard.

Detchard Every gate and door is guarded. The prisoner is never left alone. Tomorrow two regiments of Duke Michael's cavalry arrive from Strelsau. Anyone seen walking in the woods nearby is shot on sight. The roads are watched, the castle is on full alert. Take care, Madame, we have no time for double-dealers.

Antoinette No?

Detchard Rupert is waiting. You'll regret this, Madame.

Antoinette Breathing out threats and slaughter. You don't frighten me.

Detchard I might. (*Suddenly, to Rassendyll, as though to the groom*) You! Come with me. Bersonin's hungry. You can bring the food.

Detchard moves off towards the dungeons

Rassendyll and Antoinette can hardly believe their good luck

Rassendyll turns up the collar of his livery, pulls his hat well down on his head and sets off after Detchard

Antoinette vanishes into the shadows of the castle

Eerie music

The scene shifts to the dungeon where Bersonin sits guarding the King. The King lies under an old blanket—red hair just visible—at the rear of the cell. Detchard hammers on the door of the cell

Detchard Let us in! I've brought the food.

Bersonin (*hurring to open the door*) Excellent! I have an appetite this evening. (*To Rassendyll, indicating a table well down-stage of the King's bed*) Put it over there.

Detchard You're always eating. Dammit man, be hungry for a change. You'll need your appetite tomorrow.

Bersonin I haven't eaten for a day. Mama would be angry.

Detchard (*to Rassendyll*) Watch the prisoner while we eat. If he so much as moves . . . (*To Bersonin, as he joins him at the table*) He's still alive?

Bersonin (*already munching*) Last time I looked at him.

Detchard I'd like to kill him now.

Bersonin Not yet. Hentzau will tell us when.

Detchard (*after a beat*) Madame de Mauban has returned.

Bersonin How stupid of her.

Detchard Hentzau's been waiting.

Bersonin I feel sorry for the woman.

Detchard Don't. She nearly killed us earlier tonight.

They are startled by a sudden scream from somewhere in the castle above them. We can just hear the raised voices of Antoinette and Rupert in furious argument

Detchard and Bersonin get up and move to the door—then out into the corridor beyond

Detchard What the devil was that?

Bersonin A woman.

Detchard Madame de Mauban?

Bersonin Possibly. Listen . . .

Detchard Voices . . .

Bersonin An argument . . .

While they say this, Rassendyll races to the bed and shakes the King

Rassendyll (*whispering*) Your Majesty!

A groan from the King, who shifts a little, opens his eyes, sees Rassendyll . . .

On to the floor, under the bed. I'll take your place. The chains will let you. Quickly, your Majesty,—I beg you, *quickly . . . (He takes the King's place, stripping off his livery and hat, and pulling the blanket up over himself)*

Detchard (*returning*) They'll be at one another for a while.
Bersonin Then silence.

A beat. They look around. The guard has vanished

Detchard Now what the devil . . .!
Bersonin Where's he gone?
Rassendyll (*faintly, from the bed*) Food . . . food, please . . .
Detchard Did he go out?
Bersonin I told him to watch the prisoner . . .
Rassendyll A mouthful. Something . . . please . . .
Detchard What's given him a tongue . . .?
Bersonin The noise . . .
Detchard Oh shut him up . . .
Rassendyll For God's sake . . .
Bersonin (*going to the bed*) You know the rule! Silence.
Rassendyll Please . . . I beg you . . .
Bersonin You make me angry. I shall punish you.

And he sweeps the blanket off Rudolph, pulls him up by his collar, only to find himself mightily punched in the stomach and sent flying across the room

Rassendyll Good evening, gentlemen.
Detchard (*aghast*) How did you . . .
Bersonin Sacre Bleu . . .
Detchard (*furious*) Rassendyll!!
Bersonin Kill him!!

Detchard rushes to do so. A burst of gypsy music. Rassendyll has his sword ready. They fight. Furiously. Detchard is skewered, Bersonin rendered insensible. Rudolph takes the keys . . .

Rassendyll (*rushing to the King*) Your Majesty. Can you walk? I'll unchain you . . . I have the keys. . . .

He does so, but the King is too weak to walk. Rassendyll sits him on the bed. Suddenly there is another scream from above

Rassendyll seizes his sword and makes for the door

The light shifts to another part of the stage. The music swells for a moment—then . . .

Antoinette runs on—very much in déshabillé—with Rupert behind her—shirt open, passions roused

Rupert You fool. Come here!
Antoinette Get away from me!

But he catches her

Rupert You see—I simply won't allow you to say no. I have a certain obstinate, old-fashioned pride about these matters. Why should you resist Madame—when hundreds have surrendered?
Antoinette Just because of that! You gutter filth—how *dare* you . . .

Rupert forces her on to the floor. She screams

Dear God! Please help me! Michael! Michael!

Michael emerges from his room

Michael What's this . . .
Antoinette Get him away from me.
Michael Hentzau!
Rupert (*letting Antoinette go*) You seemed to have lost interest. Other matters on your mind. No time for her.
Michael How DARE you. Insolent puppy! You forget yourself!
Rupert Have a care, Michael . . .
Michael You try my patience—sir!
Rupert And you try mine. (*Quietly*) I'll tell you this. You never DO anything. Elaborate empty plans. But nothing ever happens.
Michael Be quiet.
Rupert I'm the one who does it all. One drug for King Rudolph, another for your friend—the dope-fiend here, a kidnap, a conspiracy. A fight—
Michael ENOUGH!

Rupert And when at last I've heaved you into Strelsau ON MY BACK, I'll be the one who makes it all work!

Michael (*furious*) You're not indispensable! You know what happens to people who get in my way.

Rupert *I* deal with them.

Michael Someone might deal with you!

Rupert Oh really? Who? I'd like to know . . .

Michael (*calling*) Detchard! Bersonin!

Rupert (*laughing*) No—I don't think so. Scarcely competent.

Michael Guard!! GUARD!!

Rupert I think they're all asleep.

Michael I'll do it then!

Michael lunges at Rupert with his word. Rupert easily sidesteps—skipping out of his way with infuriating elegance. As Michael stumbles, gets up, lunges again, Rupert taunts him . . .

Rupert What do you do with Antoinette I'd like to know? Do you do anything at all? Does someone else do that for you as well?

Michael DAMN YOU!

Rupert Forgive me—your Royal Highness, but we're better off without you. And my guess is—she'll be better off as well. Goodbye. Enjoy this.

Rupert draws his sword and skewers Michael rather easily. Antoinette screams and runs to him

Rupert NO! NO!!

Michael I'll tell you Rupert. I'll tell you. She and I . . . in the dark, at night—we talk. When it's very dark—we talk . . .

Antoinette Michael! Michael . . . *please*. Not yet—for my sake . . .

Michael In the dark . . .

Antoinette . . . live a little.

Michael Forever.

Michael dies

Antoinette Michael—it's dark but you must look at me. Open your eyes. Michael! (*A beat*) Don't leave me.

Rupert (*moving away*) Let's finish off the work tonight. Detchard! Bersonin! Kill the King! Finish him off—it's time. Then on to Strelsau, and the lovely Princess Flavia . . .

Rupert says this as he comes face to face with Rassendyll—on his way up from the cell

Rassendyll Good evening, Hentzau. You never gave me the fifty thousand pounds. So you see—I'm still in Ruritania.

Rupert The play actor!

Rassendyll Well—we'll play a round or two, and then I'll trouble you to pay me. After that—I'll leave you all in peace.

Rupert You'll leave us certainly—but not across the border. Say your prayers!

The big climactic duel. It should be long and spectacular. Each time Rassendyll scores a point or forces Rupert to retreat, Rupert can taunt him with ironic asides: "You're not as rusty as you look, Rassendyll" or "Be very careful, Rassendyll" or "You're beginning to try my patience". After half a dozen bouts we hear the voice of Sapt outside the castle. The fighters pause for a moment . . .

Sapt (*off*) Lower the drawbridge! In the King's name—I COMMAND YOU!

Rupert NEVER!

Rassendyll (*shouting to Sapt*) The King lives!

The fight continues. Renewed hammering on the castle gate. Rassendyll manages to force the fight towards the drawbridge. Antoinette shouts to him . . .

Antoinette RUDOLPH! The rope there! It controls the drawbridge. Cut it! Cut it!

Rassendyll Yes!

Rupert By all means, Rassendyll. And while you run to let your friends in—I'll to the King and send him to his maker! The choice is yours my friend.

A long moment. Rassendyll weighs up the situation

Rassendyll It seems I have no choice.

And he turns back to Rupert. The duel continues. Rupert is the better fighter. After another series of fierce and frantic bouts, Rassendyll is disarmed. Rupert is about to kill him, when a shot rings out. Antoinette stands—her silver derringer smoking. Rupert winces and touches blood on his shoulder, but in a moment spins and hurls a knife from his belt. Antoinette gasps and falls

Antoinette (*as she falls*) Rassendyll! The rope! The rope . . .

And with one leap he reaches the top landing and hacks at the rope. A great noise of rattling chains and the scrape of wood on wood, then a thunderous bang as the bridge falls into position

Sapt (*off; triumphantly*) We're coming in! Put down your weapons—
in the King's name . . .
Antoinette (*faintly*) An English d'Artagnan. Excellent.

Sapt and Fritz enter

Rassendyll Surrender Hentzau! You've no chance.
Rupert No chance? The devil take you, Mr Rassendyll—but I believe
my luck is in tonight. I'll wager that we meet again before too long.
Gather your strength! You'll need it. Au revoir!!

And with that he seizes the end of the cut rope and, swinging on it, leaps out and away into the night

Sapt fires a shot after him

But the urgent rhythm of a gypsy dance carries Rupert on his way

Sapt The devil!
Rassendyll Yes. The devil, Colonel Sapt.

And the scene melts into darkness and music

SCENE 8

A misty railway station in the early hours

Steam from an engine, a mournful whistle. The low growl of a train waiting to depart

Fritz hurries on. Greatcoat, scarf—but shivering nonetheless

Fritz These winter nights . . . Station master!
Station Master We're ready, sir. They've brought a special up from
Strelsau.
Fritz And REMEMBER—not a word to anyone. This is a departure
that has never happened.
Station Master (*beaming*) Yes sir! As you say. Speaking for myself, it
feels rather like a dream.

Fritz Except—one hopes—for the gold sovereign in your pocket.

Station Master Remarkable. How did it get there? Well, the things that happen . . .

Fritz Yes, yes, exactly. That's the ticket!

Station Master No. He doesn't need a ticket. Not on a Special . . .

Fritz Ha Ha! No—he wouldn't . . . Capital!

Rassendyll appears, muffled up

Rassendyll Will she come?

Fritz Sapt will bring her.

Rassendyll Yes, of course.

Fritz (*after a moment*) I'm not sure that heaven has left the right man king.

Rassendyll Don't talk like that, Fritz. You've seen what happens.

Sapt appears and, with him, Flavia

Flavia runs to Rassendyll. They embrace. Sapt and Fritz stand back

Rassendyll We managed it.

Flavia Well done.

Rassendyll A great adventure.

Flavia Yes.

Rassendyll I would have told you. Sapt interrupted me. After that there was no time. For you—I nearly left the King to die . . .

Flavia I know, I know.

Rassendyll What are we to do?

Flavia If I could come with you.

Rassendyll Ah yes. That's nice. A nice thought.

Flavia And why not? I love you. You're as good a man as he is. No. Forgive me. Better.

Rassendyll We could escape. Travel the world. Watch dolphins over the ship's rail, plant a garden, walk away together under the sky. Hide.

Flavia And be happy.

Rassendyll Yes—oh yes—we could be happy.

Flavia Far away.

Rassendyll Why don't we do it then?

Flavia You know the list. Duty, obedience, obligation.

Rassendyll Tyrants.

Flavia Honour binds me, Rudolph. And my honour keeps me here. Here with my country and my King. I have to stay.

Rassendyll That's not true. You could.

Flavia Young Rupert wasn't cruel like this. He killed things quickly.

Rassendyll A long time to die. For both of us I think.

An old, sad waltz starts to play

Flavia That morning at Falkenberg, when I felt the warm light on my hand . . .

Rassendyll And the world reared up before you like a regiment of cavalry . . .

Flavia I knew I wouldn't do justice to the day. Quite soon it would be over, and the sky would darken, and I'd think of all the things I hadn't done . . .

Rassendyll No tears. We swore. No tears.

The train whistles. Sapt coughs

My queen!

Flavia My lover and true knight. Kiss me now and go . . .

He does, they do

Wear this. (*She gives him a red rose*) Remember me.

Rassendyll Goodbye. Goodbye.

And he walks into the mist without looking back

Sapt hurries forward to support her as

The Lights fade to Black-out

FURNITURE AND PROPERTY LIST

Only essential furniture and properties, as given in the text, are listed here. Further dressing etc may be added at the Director's discretion.

ACT I

SCENE 1

On stage: Black-draped portrait of the King

Personal: **Michael:** glasses, knife, watch

SCENE 2

On stage: Daffodils
Garden furniture

Personal: **Rassendyll:** fencing foil
Harry: fencing foil
Robert: *The Times*

SCENE 3

Personal: **Rupert:** brandy bottle

SCENE 4

Personal: **Rassendyll:** luggage
Small child: Baedecker
Antoinette: Valise. *In it:* tickets, papers, small gun

SCENE 5

On stage: Empty bottles

SCENE 6/7

Personal: **Rassendyll:** haversack, papers
Stand-in: binoculars, haversack
Sapt: rifle
Fritz: rifle
Rudolph: gun

SCENE 8

No props required

SCENE 9

On stage: High-backed settle
Chairs
Hunting trophies
Bottles
Glasses

Off stage: Full bottles **(Josef)**
Old dusty bottle on tray **(Josef)**

SCENE 10

Personal: **Antoinette:** candle

SCENE 11

Off-stage: Bucket of water **(Sapt)**

SCENE 12

No props required

SCENE 13

No props required

SCENE 14

No props required

ACT II

SCENE 1

On stage: Coloured lanterns

SCENE 2

On stage: Table
Candle
Large sabre

Personal: **Rassendyll:** matches
Sapt: revolver
Detchard: sabre
Bersonin: sabre

SCENE 3

On stage: Deep armchair

Personal: **Rupert:** bottle

SCENE 4

On stage: Photograph album

Off stage: Note **(Flavia)**

SCENE 5

On stage: Racks of clothes
Vats of water
Washing boards, lines, blocks of soap
One clothes line with sheets

Personal: **Rassendyll:** revolver

SCENE 6

Personal: **Flavia:** red rose

SCENE 7

On stage: Bed, blanket

Off stage: Tray of food **(Rassendyll)**

Personal: **Bersonin:** keys
Rassendyll: sabre
Michael: sabre
Antoinette: small gun (derringer)
Rupert: sabre, knife

SCENE 8

Personal: **Flavia:** rose

LIGHTING PLOT

ACT I, SCENE 1

To open: Torchlight

Cue 1   **Sapt** goes. Music fades   (Page 5)
           Lights fade

ACT I, SCENE 2

To open: Bright Spring light

Cue 2   **Rassendyll:** "I'll do my best.". Music   (Page 9)
           Lights change

ACT I, SCENE 3

To open: Night

Cue 3   **Rupert:** ". . . your Royal Highness."   (Page 12)
           Black-out

ACT I, SCENE 4

To open: Spot on Rassendyll

Cue 4   **Rassendyll:** ". . . and inexplicable encounters."   (Page 12)
           Lights up on station platform

Cue 5   **Rassendyll:** "And good luck!" Music swells   (Page 15)
           Fade to black-out

ACT I, SCENE 5

To open: Interior

Cue 6   **Sapt:** "Thank you my dear. Thank you."   (Page 18)
           Crossfade to Scene 6/7

ACT I, SCENE 6/7

To open: Heavily dappled sunlight

Cue 7   As stand-in goes to sleep   (Page 20)
           Lights indicate passage of time

Cue 8   **Sapt:** ". . . stuff him with chestnuts".   (Page 23)
           Lights fade

ACT I, SCENE 8

To open: Night. Firelight

Cue 9   **Antoinette:** "Rupert! Rupert."   (Page 25)
           Lights fade

ACT I, SCENE 9

To open: Night. Firelight

Cue 10   **Fritz** and **Sapt** fall in a drunken sleep   (Page 28)
           Fade to black-out. Then up on Scene 10

ACT I, SCENE 10

To open: Night. Interior

Cue 11   **Michael** and **Antoinette** exit   (Page 30)
           Fade to black-out

ACT I, SCENE 11

To open: Early morning light

Cue 12   Music whirls   (Page 30)
           Fade lights

ACT I, SCENE 12

To open: Interior. Daylight

Cue 13   **Flavia:** "Just as you like it."   (Page 35)
           Fast fade to black-out

ACT I, Scene 13

To open: Exterior. Daylight

Cue 14 **Strakencz:** ". . . into the Cathedral, Sire." (Page 36)
Lights cross-fade to Scene 14

ACT I, Scene 14

To open: Interior. Cathedral. Candles

Cue 15 Anthem finishes (Page 37)
Lights dim

Cue 16 Group turn to face out front (Page 38)
Lights up on group

Cue 17 **Rassendyll** waves to crowd (Page 38)
Lights burn brightly then fade to black-out

ACT II, Scene 1

To open: Exterior. Night. Candlelight, lighted lanterns

Cue 18 **Flavia:** "Good night, Madame." (Page 47)
Fade to black-out

ACT II, Scene 2

To open: Darkness. Moonlight

Cue 19 **Rassendyll** lights the candle (Page 48)
Bring up covering spots

Cue 20 **Rassendyll** extinguishes the candle (Page 50)
Cut covering spots

Cue 21 **Detchard** and **Bersonin** enter with lanterns (Page 50)
Bring up covering spots

ACT II, Scene 3

To open: Crossfade from previous scene

Cue 22 Sinister music (Page 54)
Lights flicker

Cue 23 Music creeps up (Page 54)
Black-out

ACT II, Scene 4

To open: Interior

Cue 24	**Rassendyll:** "I'd better hurry."	(Page 59)
	Lights fade	

ACT II, Scene 5

To open: Darkness. Moonlight with covering spots

Cue 25	**Rupert:** "I *say*". Music swirls	(Page 63)
	Fade to black-out	

ACT II, Scene 6

To open: Candlelight. Torchlight

No cues

ACT II, Scene 7

To open: Crossfade from Scene 6

Cue 26	Scene change to dungeon	(Page 68)
	Lights change	
Cue 27	**Rassendyll** makes for the door	(Page 70)
	Light shifts to another part of the stage	
Cue 28	**Rassendyll:** "The devil, Colonel Sapt."	(Page 73)
	Fade to black-out	

ACT II, Scene 8

To open: Exterior. Early morning light

Cue 29	**Sapt** supports **Flavia**	(Page 75)
	Fade to black-out	

EFFECTS PLOT

Music cues are not included in this plot. Please see the note about incidental music in the Production Note page vi

ACT I

Cue 1   **Robert:** "Do you promise?"   (Page 9)
Rudolph's name is called faintly

Cue 2   **Rupert:** "And a couple of mountains."   (Page 10)
Echo effect

Cue 3   **Rupert:** "His name's Rudolph . . ."   (Page 10)
Distant crash

Cue 4   **Rupert:** " . . . your Royal Highness." Black-out   (Page 12)
Train rushes through, whistle shrieks. Continue train noise under Rassendyll's speech

Cue 5   **Rassendyll:** ". . . superb account of Don Giovanni."   (Page 12)
Cut train noise. Few bars of Don Giovanni which fades into busy station concourse, the opera being picked up by a barrel organ

Cue 6   **Antoinette:** "No buts, Mr Rassendyll."   (Page 14)
Train whistle

Cue 7   To open Scene 6
Waterfall. Birdsong

Cue 8   **Rassendyll:** "Halloo."   (Page 18)
Echo effect

Cue 9   Stand-in goes to sleep   (Page 20)
Chorus of rooks

Cue 10   (optional) **Rudolph:** ". . . enjoy ourselves this evening."   (Page 22)
Sounds of boar as script with gun shot

Cue 11   **Michael:** "Yes . . . Yes . . ."   (Page 29)
Four o'clock bells

Cue 12   To open Scene 11   (Page 30)
            Cock crows. Dawn chorus

Cue 13   To open Scene 12   (Page 33)
            Crowd noises, brass band in distance

Cue 14   **Michael:** ". . . into place. And then . . ."   (Page 35)
            Clock chimes prior to hour striking. The hour strokes as cued
            p. 35 with cheers after fifth stroke

Cue 15   **Flavia:** "Just as you like it."   (Page 35)
            Riot of bells, cheering

Cue 16   **Sapt** signals   (Page 36)
            Crowd cheers

Cue 17   To open Scene 14   (Page 37)
            Incense

Cue 18   Lights up on group   (Page 38)
            Roar of applause, cheers, bells, petals falling

ACT II

Cue 19   To open Act II   (Page 39)
            Distant ballroom chatter

Cue 20   **Flavia:** "Good night, Madame."   (Page 47)
            Thunder of hooves and carriage wheels

Cue 21   **Rassendyll** and **Sapt** enter darkened room   (Page 48)
            Clock ticks. Continue through scene

Cue 22   **Sapt:** "God save the King!!"   (Page 51)
            Shot rings out

Cue 23   To open Scene 7   (Page 66)
            Horses galloping, carriage wheels, drawbridge as per script

Cue 24   **Rupert** prepares to kill **Rassendyll**   (Page 72)
            Shot rings out

Cue 25   **Rassendyll** hacks the rope   (Page 73)
            Rattling chains, scrape of wood on wood, thunderous bang

Cue 26   To open Scene 8   (Page 73)
            Mist. Steam from train. Mournful whistle. Growl of train

Cue 27   **Rassendyll:** "No tears." (2nd time)   (Page 75)
            Train whistles